WORD AS MANTRA

The Art of Raja Rao

OUR RECENT RELEASES

Short Fiction

Katha Prize Stories 12
  Ed Geeta Dharmarajan
Best of the Nineties:
Katha Prize Stories 11
  Ed Geeta Dharmarajan
The End of Human History
  By Hasan Manzar
Hauntings: Bangla Ghost Stories
  Ed and Trans by
  Suchitra Samanta
Forsaking Paradise: Stories from Ladakh,
  Ed and Trans by
  Ravina Aggarwal
Ayoni and Other Stories
  Ed and Trans by
  Alladi Uma & M Sridhar
Home and Away
  By Ramachandra Sharma
  Trans by Padma and
  Ramachandra Sharma

ALT (Approaches to Literatures in Translation)

Ismat: Her Life, Her Times
  Eds Sukrita Paul Kumar & Sadique
Translating Partition
  Eds Ravikant & Tarun K Saint
Translating Caste
  Ed Tapan Basu
Translating Desire
  Ed Brinda Bose
Vijay Tendulkar

Trailblazers

Ambai: Two Novellas and a Story
  Trans by C T Indra,
  Prema Seetharam & Uma Narayanan

Paul Zacharia: Two Novellas
  Trans by Gita Krishnankutty
Ashokamitran: Water
  Trans by Lakshmi Holmström
Bhupen Khakhar: Selected Works
  Trans by Bina Srinivasan,
  Ganesh Devy & Naushil Mehta,
Indira Goswami: Pages Stained with Blood
  Trans by Pradip Acharya

Katha Classics

Pudumaippittan
  Ed Lakshmi Holmström
Basheer Ed Vanajam Ravindran
Mauni Ed Lakshmi Holmström
Raja Rao Ed Makarand Paranjape
A Madhaviah Padmavati
  Trans Meenakshi Tyagarajan

Katha Novels

Singarevva and the Palace
  By Chandrasekhar Kambar
  Trans by Laxmi Chandrashekar
Listen Girl!
  By Krishna Sobti
  Trans by Shivanath

YuvaKatha

Lukose's Church
Night of the Third Crescent
Bhiku's Diary
The Verdict
The Dragonfly
The Bell

Forthcoming

Links in Our Chain
  By Mahadevi Verma
  Trans by Neera Kuckreja Sohoni
Mountain of the Moon
  By Bibhutibhushan Bandopadhyay
  Trans by Santanu Sinha Chaudhuri

WORD AS MANTRA

The Art of Raja Rao

Edited by
Robert L Hardgrave, Jr

A Katha Profile

KATHA

First published by Katha in 1998　　KATHA
in association with the Center for　　A3 Sarvodaya Enclave
Asian Studies, the University of　　Sri Aurobindo Marg,
Texas at Austin　　New Delhi 110 017
　　Phone: 2652 4350, 2652 4511
　　Fax: 2651 4373

The collection as a whole © 1998 Katha
The individual contributions　　E-mail: kathavilasam@katha.org
© 1998 the respective authors　　Internet address: www.katha.org

KATHA is a registered nonprofit society
devoted to enhancing the pleasures of reading.
KATHA VILASAM is its story research and resource centre.

General Series Editor: Geeta Dharmarajan
In-house Editors: Chandana Dutta, Dipli Saikia,
Nandita Aggarwal, Sridala Swami

Cover Design: Arvinder Chawla

Typeset in 10.5 on 14pt ElegaGaramond BT by Sandeep Kumar,
Suresh Sharma at Katha
Printed at Usha Offset, New Delhi

All rights reserved. No part of this book may be reproduced or utilized in any
form or by any means, electronic or mechanical, including photocopying,
recording or by any information storage or retrieval system, without the
prior written permission of the publisher.

ISBN 81-85586-83-7

3 5 7 9 10 8 6 4 2

CONTENTS

Preface
   Robert L Hardgrave, Jr

Acknowledgements

Raja Rao: A Personal Tribute   1
   Kathleen Raine

The Example of Raja Rao   6
   R Parthasarathy

Raja Rao, Teacher   38
   Robert D King

Raja Rao: Each Work a Magic Casement   51
   C D Narasimhaiah

Raja Rao: Madhyama and Mantra   60
   Braj B Kachru

Context, Creativity, Style: Strategies in Raja Rao's Novels   88
   Yamuna Kachru

The Difficult Pilgrimage:
The Chessmaster and His Moves **and its Readers**   108
   Makarand Paranjape

Raja Rao: Master of Language, Rigveda 10.81.7   133
    Winfred P Lehmann

Blinding I: Toward a Poetics of
Post-Traditional Technology   142
    Raman Srinivasan

Presentation of the Sahitya Akademi
Fellowship to Raja Rao   169
    U R Anantha Murthy

Acceptance Speech   174
    Raja Rao

Chronology
Selected Bibliography
Interview with Raja Rao
    Anne Morris
About the Contributors

Publication of *Word as Mantra* has been made possible, in part, by a grant from the Marlene and Morton Meyerson Chair for South Asian Studies at the University of Texas at Austin.

PREFACE

For more than thirty years, Raja Rao has honoured the University of Texas at Austin as a member of its faculty and, in retirement, by his continued involvement in the intellectual life of the community. The University, in recognition of his contributions, honoured Raja Rao at a one-day symposium, "Word as Mantra: The Art of Raja Rao," on 24 March, 1997. Organized by the Center for Asian Studies in cooperation with the Harry H Ransom Humanities Research Center, the symposium brought scholars and friends from around the world to celebrate and honour Raja Rao as author, philosopher, teacher and mentor. The symposium was supported by the Marlene and Morton Meyerson Centennial Chair in Asian Studies at the University of Texas and assisted by the Rockefeller Foundation.

Born in Mysore State in South India in 1908, Raja Rao was educated in India and continued his studies in French language and literature at the University of Montpellier and the Sorbonne. While in France as a student, he began writing in his native Kannada and in French, but settled on English as his major medium of expression. His first novel, *Kanthapura*, was published in 1938 in London. Among the novels and stories that followed, *The Serpent and the Rope*, 1960, brought him recognition not only as one of India's greatest writers, but, without regard to nationality, as a master of English prose. In 1969, the Government of India honoured Rao with the prestigious Padma Bhushan and in 1988, he became the tenth recipient of the Neustadt International Prize for Literature.

Raja Rao joined the faculty of the Department of Philosophy at the University of Texas in 1965, teaching courses on Indian religion and philosophy. He retired as Professor Emeritus in 1980, and resides with his wife Susan in Austin.

The symposium "Word as Mantra," honouring Raja Rao, provided the occasion for the Sahitya Akademi to present Rao with its Fellowship, the highest honour conferred by the Akademi on any Indian writer and one reserved for those who have achieved the greatest distinction in the world of letters. The then President of the Akademi, U R Anantha Murthy, made the presentation. "At eighty eight, Rao is one of the most innovative novelists now writing," Anantha Murthy said. "Departing boldly from the European tradition of the novel, [Rao] explores the metaphysical basis of writing itself, and of the world through his works of fiction. His concern is with the human condition rather than with a particular nation or people. Writing to him is sadhana, a form of spiritual growth. That is why he would go on writing even if he were alone in the world."

The papers of the symposium, included in this volume, explore the world and word of Raja Rao through various themes. Robert D King provides a personal insight into Rao as a teacher. C D Narasimhaiah, R Parthasarathy, Yamuna Kachru and Braj B Kachru address Rao's work as a whole, especially his masterly use of English as a language of India. Makarand Paranjape focuses on *The Chessmaster and His Moves*, and Winfred P Lehmann takes the Rigveda as a vehicle to examine Rao's use of language. Raman Srinivasan relates the work of Raja Rao to "a poetics of post-traditional technology." Edwin Thumboo, of the National University of Singapore, participated in the symposium, with a paper entitled "*The Cat and Shakespeare*: Words with Nine Lives," that we were unable to include in this volume.

The efforts of many people went into the success of the symposium and in the preparation of this volume. I would like to thank Jeannie Cortez, Administrative Assistant for the Center for Asian Studies, for her logistical work in symposium arrangements, and Anne Alexander, Adminsitrative Associate for the Center, for her assistance in preparing the papers for publication. Finally, I would like to thank Katha for making the publication of this volume possible.

The University of Texas at Austin   Robert L Hardgrave, Jr
November, 1998

ACKNOWLEDGEMENTS

Katha takes immense pleasure in thanking Professor Raja Rao and his wife, Susan Raja Rao, for giving us the opportunity to commemorate his ninetieth birthday with this collection of essays. We wish him good health and every happiness.

We are very grateful to Professor Robert L Hardgrave, Jr, of the University of Texas at Austin, USA, editor of the volume, and to its contributors, U R Anantha Murthy, Anne Morris, Braj B Kachru, Kathleen Raine, Makarand Paranjape, C D Narasimhaiah, R Parthasarathy, Raman Srinivasan, Robert D King, Winfred P Lehmann and Yamuna Kachru.

Katha would also like to thank *World Literature Today*, the University of Oklahoma, the photographer Gil Jain and Prof C D Narasimhaiah for providing us with valuable photographs for this volume.

KATHLEEN RAINE
RAJA RAO:
A PERSONAL TRIBUTE

It was, I think, in 1983, a conference at the India International Centre in New Delhi, at which delegates from the West met some of the best minds in India – then unknown to me, but who have since become valued and honoured friends – that I first met Raja Rao. One of our English delegates, Paul Sharrad, had been putting forward a Christian (Orthodox) statement. Raja Rao, hitherto silent, uncoiled himself and asked, "Will you please tell me what you mean by the word God?" At that moment I knew that I had reached India, and my heart said, "Home at last." Western answers were themselves questions.

A few days later Raja Rao invited me to lunch with him and opened the door to India a little wider. "India," he said, "is not a nation, like France or Italy or Germany: India is a state of being" (or perhaps the word he used was "mind" or "consciousness": of the word I am uncertain, but I understood the meaning). India, Raja Rao implied, is open to whoever can attain it, and his words spoke to me like an invitation. When, in his novel, *The Serpent and the Rope*, I read further, "India lies beyond sorrow," I understood that "India" – the eternal India, the India of the Imagination, that supreme civilization laden with the wisdom and the beauty of millennia – is the end to which those long journeys, lifetimes, all inevitably lead: India is indeed "Home at last."

At that time Kamaladevi Chattopadhyay – great patriot and friend of Gandhiji – was President of the India International Centre. Woman of the theatre, lover of the performing arts, she had worked tirelessly for Indian craftspeople since Independence, establishing in every major town, emporia where a fair price was paid for their work; resettling refugees from Pakistan after Partition; and above all, working for women, enabling them to contribute their skills and obtain proper recognition. Kamaladeviji received me with friendship and from her I learned much about modern India. Who, I asked her, were the significant writers? She named only one, Raja Rao, as India's greatest novelist. I read *Kanthapura*, his first novel, whose theme is the struggle for Independence in a South Indian village, and especially the contribution of the women. I then read *The Serpent and the Rope*, and understood that Raja Rao is more than a novelist; he is a philosopher who uses the novel as a vehicle to explore profound themes and to illuminate his vision of the "India" of the mind. He is qualified to do so to a rare degree, having studied both at the Sorbonne and at the University of Montpellier; his first wife was French, and his cultural formation was French rather than English. He has continued to spend periods in France. In *The Serpent and the Rope* he compares "India" with Western Christendom at a very profound level. He later told me that at one time Catholic monasticism and Scholastic theology had so attracted him that he had seriously thought of entering a monastic order. Thus he came to understand Europe, not through England, but at a higher and more subtle intellectual level, mainly through France and through the great Catholic theological tradition.

At the beginning of this century, the West knew little of Indian thought, with the exception of the Theosophical movement. Western confidence in its materialist science – whose impressive discoveries and inventions in the field of technology have been so prestigious – went unchallenged. No alternative was seriously considered. Raja Rao was therefore among the first to present the "India of the Imagination" to Western readers as a great civilization grounded in totally other premises than those of the West. To the Western mind it seems self-evident that reality is the world we perceive, an "object" external to the observer; to India, it is no less self-evident that the perceiving mind is the ground, and reality not an "object" but a living experience. The difference, finally, is between a lifeless and a living world; the final result of the Western view is to reduce all life to mechanism devoid of meaning or value, to, ultimately, a nihil. The Vedic world is a living world, its ground sat-chit-ananda (being-consciousness-bliss) of essential existence. Deeply as he has respected Western spirituality, Raja Rao has never doubted the more fundamental understanding which underlies the Vedic tradition and is the inspiration of the philosophy and the arts of Indian civilization, flowering in sculpture and dance, mathematics and architecture, painting and music and poetry; all alike grounded in the sacred nature of things.

Meanwhile we had become friends; I had published in *Temenos*, which I edited during the 1980s, an essay by Raja Rao on "The Ultimate Word."

> So there is only one poet: The "I" of the I. The atman beyond jiva. He is no one. He is. Is, is. And so it. Call It, Brahman, if you like.
> The *Vakyapadiya* says, "the Brahman who is without beginning or end, whose very essence is the Word (sabda), who is the cause of the manifested phonemes, who appears as the objects, from whom the creation of the world (seems to) proceed ..." Thus begins the *Vakyapadiya*, the celebrated text on the Phrase and the Word.[1]
>
> Sanctification is dissolution. Time burnt is poetry made. When time and place are burnt to ash – that is the concrete object is – only light shines over.[2]

Powerful words that challenge our Western understanding at the very root.

The Chessmaster and His Moves, awarded the prestigious Neustadt Laureate prize in 1988, is a further exploration of the differences between the European and the Indian mind, the Indian and European attitudes to love. Raja Rao especially considers the other great spiritual tradition, that of the Jews. Raja Rao has made his home in Austin, Texas, and had in 1988 already married his present (American) wife, and has completed a further novel (not yet published) exploring the American experience. Yet as he explores the West, so at the same time he enters ever more deeply into that "India" which can only be the ultimate reality, both for the East and the West. He has long been a devotee of an Indian teacher of the purest Vedic tradition, visiting India every year and spending time at his Master's ashram, with his wife Susan. His health now prevents him from returning to live in India, his spiritual home; but it has been his destiny to open up a profound insight into that eternal India, for many Western readers. In this his word stands in contrast to the many new Indian novelists who see India through Westernized eyes.

At the beginning of this century, the West (with a few exceptions, like the American Transcendentalists, and later the Theosophical Society), never doubting the supremacy of Western civilization, poured missionaries into the most civilized land on earth, where they were tolerated, within a culture that knows no dogma. Now the tide is flowing the other way – the West looking to the East, to India and to Buddhist countries, for spiritual knowledge. Raja Rao would make no claim to be a spiritual teacher – he is, on the contrary, himself a Devotee – but his novels are profound explorations of the interaction of the two contrasting civilizations from the standpoint of a follower of the Indian dharma, revealing the majestic grandeur of the universe which opens for whoever attains that "India" which is not a country but a state of being.

Notes

1. Raja Rao. "The Ultimate Word." *The Meaning of India*. New Delhi: Vision Books, 1996. 162-63.
2. ibid 160.

R PARTHASARATHY

THE EXAMPLE OF RAJA RAO

In 1929, a young Brahmin from Hyderabad, India, set out for France, for Montpellier in fact, "that ancient Greek and Saracenic town, so close to Séte where Valéry was born,"[1] at the invitation of Sir Patrick Geddes who had established the Collège des Ecossais there. It was, however, at Soissons where Abelard was imprisoned and condemned that the Brahmin, Raja Rao, wrote his first stories, "Javni" and "The Little Gram Shop." *Kanthapura* was, for the most part, written in a thirteenth century French castle in the Alps, and published in London in 1938 by Allen and Unwin.

The following year, Rao was back in India, a sadhaka (aspirant) in Ramana Maharshi's ashram in Tiruvannamalai, Madras Presidency. "Unless you be a pilgrim you will never know yourself."[2] And so, in his search for a guru, he wandered in and out of the ashrams of Sri Aurobindo and Gandhi. His journey ended in 1943 in Tiruvananthapuram when he met Sri Atmananda Guru. For the next seventeen years, he lived in India and France. In 1947, Roy Hawkins of Oxford University Press, Bombay, published *The Cow of the Barrricades and Other Stories*. Rao's spiritual experiences as a Vedantin form the basis of his next two novels, *The Cat and Shakespeare*, published as "The Cat" in the summer 1959 issue of *Chelsea Review*, and in 1965 by Macmillan, and *The Serpent and the Rope*, published in 1960 by John Murray.

Rao moved to Austin, Texas, in 1966 to begin teaching Indian philosophy at the University of Texas, a position he held until his retirement in 1980. In 1978, as his editor at Oxford University Press, Madras, I published *The Policeman and the Rose: Stories*. Meanwhile, in 1965, Rao's fourth novel, *Comrade Kirillov*, had appeared in a French translation in Paris. And finally, in 1988, exactly fifty years after the publication of his first novel, Kapil Malhotra of Vision Books, New Delhi published *The Chessmaster and His Moves*, the first volume of a trilogy, to be followed by *The Daughter of the Mountain* and *A Myrobalan in the Palm of Your Hand*. Rao was awarded the tenth Neustadt International Prize for Literature in 1988.

At ninety, Rao is one of the most innovative novelists now writing. Departing boldly from the European tradition of the novel, he has indigenized it in the process of assimilating material from the Indian literary tradition. He has put the novel to uses to which it had not perhaps been put before by exploring the metaphysical basis of writing itself; of, in fact, the word.

As a writer, Rao's concern is with the human condition rather than with a particular nation or ethnic group. "One of the disciplines that has interested me in Indian literature," Rao told me one pleasant February morning in Adayar, Chennai,

> ... is its sense of sadhana (*exercitia spiritualia*)– a form of spiritual growth. In that sense, one is alone in the world. I can say that all I write is for myself. If I were to live in a forest, I would still go on writing. If I were to live anywhere else, I would still go on writing, because I enjoy the magic of the word. That magic is cultivated mainly by inner silence, one that is cultivated not by associating oneself with society

> but often by being away from it. I think I try to belong to the great Indian tradition of the past when literature was considered a sadhana. In fact, I wanted to publish my books anonymously because I think they do not belong to me. But my publisher refused."[3]

The house of fiction that Rao has built is thus founded on the metaphysical and linguistic speculations of the Indians. It is to the masters of fiction in our time, such as Proust and Joyce, that we must ultimately turn for a writer of comparable stature.

One of the difficulties a reader encounters in the presence of South Asian literature in English is that of understanding the nature of the world projected by the text, and by implication the strategies of discourse adopted by the writer to nativize the English language. Not enough attention has so far been paid to this in the South Asian context, with the exception of Braj Kachru's study.[4] Kachru examines the problem from the perspective of a sociolinguist. I will, however, try to explore its implications generally in the context of South Asian literature in English, and specifically in the context of the fiction of Raja Rao. His fiction offers a paradigm of South Asian literature in English with all its contradictions.

The Foreword to *Kanthapura* is revolutionary in its declaration of independence from English literature, and has, as a result, become a classic stylistic guide for non-native English writers everywhere:

> There is no village in India, however mean, that has not a rich sthalapurana, or legendary history, of its own. Some god or god-like hero has passed by the village ... the Mahatma himself, on one of his many pilgrimages through the country, might have slept in this hut, the low one, by the village gate. In this way the past mingles with the present, and the gods mingle with men to make the repertory of your grandmother always bright. One such story from the contemporary annals of my village I have tried to tell.[5]

Kanthapura is the story of how Gandhi's struggle for Independence from the British came to an unknown village in South India. The struggle takes the form, on the one hand, of nonviolent resistance to Pax Britannica and, on the other, of a social protest to reform Indian society. References to specific events in India in the late 1920s and the early 1930s suggest that the novel has grown out of a distinct historical context. Told by an old woman, Achakka, the story evokes the spirit and discourse of the traditional folk narratives, the Puranas. It is sixty years since Rao wrote that Foreword. In an attempt to elucidate Rao's intentions, I shall examine the Foreword as an introduction to his own fiction.

Since the rise of the novel in the eighteenth century, its philosophical bias has been toward the particular; hence, its focus on the individual in an objective world. An entirely opposite view is expressed in *The Serpent and the Rope*: India is "perhaps the only nation that throughout history has questioned the existence of the world – of the object."[6] When a non-native English writer, such as Rao, chooses this specific genre rather than one that is traditional to his own culture, the epic, for instance, and further chooses to project this genre in a second language, he takes upon himself the burden of synthesizing the projections of both cultures. Out of these circumstances, Rao has forged what I consider a truly exemplary style in South Asian English, in fact in World English, literature. He has, above all, tried to show how the spirit of one culture can be possessed by, and communicated in, another language.

English as a code is now universally shared by both native and non-native speakers. What are not always shared or recognized are the manifestations of a specific culture embedded by the writer in the language. Though the language can now be taken for granted, what cannot any longer be taken for granted are the cultural deposits transmitted by the language. To understand them the reader, especially if he is a native speaker, must equip himself with a knowledge of the writer's sociocultural milieu. Would he not be expected to do so if he were to read an English translation of, say, the Mahabharata or, for that matter, the Iliad?

Culture determines literary form, and the form of the novel from cultures within South Asia has been strongly influenced by those cultures themselves, resulting in something different from the form of the novel in the West. Rao himself is of the opinion that an Indian can never write a novel; he can only write a Purana. The Puranas are sacred history included in the canon of scripture, and they tell stories of the origin of the universe, the exploits of gods and heroes, and the genealogies of kings. Their impact on the minds and imaginations of the people of India has been profound. Through them the Vedas and the Upanishads and the ideas of the great tradition of Hinduism were communicated by intention and organized effort to the people, and woven into their lives in festivals and rituals. The Mahabharata and the Ramayana were expressly composed for the same purpose. There is, at least in Southern India, an unbroken tradition of recitation of the two epics by ruler and teacher in the vernacular languages. The epics were recited in the form of stories by the sutapauranikas, bards who recite the Puranas.

Sanskrit is, in fact, an obsession with Rao: "It is the source of our culture ... and I have wished a thousand times that I had written in Sanskrit."[7] Intellectually and emotionally, he is deeply rooted in the Indian tradition, especially in the philosophical tradition of the Advaita Vedanta of Sankara (8th century CE). Sankara was interested in the nature of the relationship of the individual self (atman) with the universal Self (Brahman). He insisted that they were identical (tat tvam asi, "You are That")[8], and that all appearances of plurality and difference arose from the false interpretation of the data presented by the mind and senses. He therefore rejected subject-object dualism. The only reality is Brahman. For Sankara, liberation (moksa) was the ultimate aim, and he defined it as intuitive knowledge of the identity of atman and Brahman, and not, it is to be remembered, union with God.

Rao's ideas of language, especially the empowerment of the word, are formed by the linguistic speculations of the Indians, notably Patanjali (2nd century BCE). This is what Patanjali says in his classic formulation of the view in his great commentary on the Grammar [*Vyakarana Mahabhasya*] of Panini: "A single word, well used and perfectly understood and conforming to the sacred texts, is in heaven and in the world the sacred cow to fulfill every wish."[9] In the Indian tradition, literature (sahitya) was a way of realizing the Absolute (Brahman) through the mediation of language. "Therefore, the attainment of faultless speech," states Bhartrhari (5th century CE) in the *Vakyapadiya* [Of the Sentence and the Word] "is the attainment of Brahman. He who knows the secret of its functioning enjoys the immortal Brahman."[10] The literary artefact in itself had no significance. It was this metaphysical bias that distinguished Indian literature from every other literature.

Again, there is a long tradition in Indian literature of the use of silence (maunam) as an effective means of expression. The possibilities of the unspoken word are exploited to the full. Its use stems from a recognition that language is limited in its expressive resources. There are usually four levels ascribed to language: 1. Para, transcendent, and thus inaccessible; 2. Pasyanti, illuminated, but still on the transcendent plane; 3. Madhyama, mentally articulated; and 4. Vaikhari, the language of everyday discourse. The first three levels concern themselves with the ineffable. The word is born in the fullness of silence, and this fullness confers on the word its legitimate function. Behind silence is the absolute word (paravac) to which, through silence, words move. Louis Renou has stated this explicitly with reference to the Vedas: "In a work of this kind it is silence, the inexpressible, which is more important than the thing uttered, whence derives the essential role of the Brahman as the officiant of silence."[11] It therefore follows that the writer has to learn, not so much to speak as to listen, to listen to himself with total attention. Rao himself observes:

> ... to say a flower ... you must be able to say it in such a way that the force of the vocable has the power to create the flower. Unless word becomes mantra, no writer is a writer, and no reader a reader ... We in India need but to recognize our inheritance. Let us never forget Bhartrhari.[12]

Mantra may be understood either as an instrument of thought (<man, to think + tra, a suffix used to make words denote instruments) or as salvific thought (< man, to think + trai, to save; mananat trayate ity mantrah, by whose thinking one is saved, that is mantra). Mantra as salvific thought is expressed in the well-known formula:

> Mananam sarvaveditvam trenam samsarasagarat /
> mananatranadharmavan mantra ity abhidhiyate //[13]
> The mantra is so called because it is in the nature of thought and deliverance.
> It is indeed all-knowing thought and release from transmigration.[14]

In an oral culture, such as that of the Indians, thinking is done mnemonically to facilitate oral recurrence. Thought comes into existence in rhythmic, balanced patterns, in repetitions or antitheses, in epithetic, aphoristic or formulaic utterances, in proverbs, or in other mnemonic forms. Words are therefore invested with power, and this relates them to the sacral, to the ultimate concerns of existence.

In examining Rao's use of English it is important to keep in mind his philosophical and linguistic orientations. The house of fiction that he has built rests on these twin foundations. Amongst South Asian writers in English he is perhaps unique in his attempt not only to nativize, but also to Sanskritize, the English language. Sanskritization is used here in the sense it is understood by anthropologists as a process of social and cultural change in Indian civilization. Rao strains to the limit all the expressive resources of the language. As a result, the Indian reality that emerges from his writing is authentic. Foremost among the problems that the South Asian writer has to wrestle with are, first, the expression of modes of thinking and feeling specific to his culture, and second, terminology. Rao overcomes the first problem by invariably drawing upon Kannada and Sanskrit, and in the process he uses devices like loan translation, idiomatic and syntactic equivalences, and the imitation of native-style repertoires. He overcomes the second problem of finding words for culturally bound objects by contextualizing them so that their meanings are self-evident. By evoking the necessary cultural ambience, these strategies help the writer to be part of the mainstream of the literatures of India.

In an illuminating essay investigating the nature of the Russian poet Osip Mandelstam's Jewishness, Arthur Cohen observes:

> A poet's nation is his language and unless one wills to become of no language or of several languages or to put on languages without fixity of place, the poet has no choice but to become the language he speaks and hopefully, if one is great in the use of the language, to change it as profoundly as one is changed. But language by itself is not a nation, however much the experience of the people is transmitted through its unfolding, resonation, and echo. Language is abstract until it becomes one's own language and then it is possessed, most particularly.[15]

Among Kannada, Sanskrit, French, and English, it is English that Rao most consummately possesses, and it is in that language that his fiction most consummately speaks to us. From the beginning, English is ritually de-anglicized. In *Kanthapura*, English is thick with the agglutinants of Kannada; in *The Serpent and the Rope*, the Indo-European kinship between English and Sanskrit is creatively exploited; and in *The Cat and Shakespeare*, English is made to approximate the rhythm of Sanskrit chants. At the apex of this linguistic pyramid is *The Chessmaster and His Moves*, wherein Rao has perfected an idiolect uniquely and inimitably his own. It is the culmination of his experiments with the English language spanning more than fifty years. *The Chessmaster and His Moves* has none of the self-consciousness in the use of English that characterizes his other work. In it he realizes the style that had eluded him in *The Serpent and the Rope*. Of style, he writes:

> The style of a man ... the way he weaves word against word, intricates the existence of sentences with the values of

sound, makes a comma here, puts a dash there: all are signs of the inner movement, the speed of his life, his breath (prana), the nature of his thought, the ardour and age of his soul. (1960: 164-65)

A peasant society, such as Kanthapura's, has a homogeneous outlook and tradition. Its relationship to tradition produces a sense of unity and continuity between the present and past generations. Tradition is therefore an important instrument in ensuring social interdependence. Under the Raj, even villages weren't spared the blessings of Pax Britannica. It triggered socioeconomic changes that eventually split up the small communities. The oral tradition itself became fragmented, though it remained the chronicler of the motherland through a poetically gifted individual's repertoire.

Kanthapura is a mine of information about the sociocultural life of peasant society in Southern India. This is usually the perspective from which the novel is read in the West – the little tradition pitted against the great tradition, to use the terms proposed by Robert Redfield.[16] Redfield distinguishes the beliefs and practices of the folk from those of the elite in an agrarian society. The little tradition functions as a symbolic criticism of the great tradition, while at the same time gravitating toward it because of the latter's institutional charisma. Brahmins, for instance, who sit atop the caste hierarchy, owe their status to the belief that they alone are empowered to perform the samskaras, central rituals, of Hinduism. The recognition by peasants of a great tradition, of which their practices are a variant, implies a stratification of culture. In a complex society such as India the stratification of culture implies a stratification of power and wealth. The representatives of the great tradition are the gentry, officials, and priests who collectively form a ruling as well as a cultural elite. Relations between the little and great traditions are uneasy, and fraught with tension as their interests are diametrically opposed. The existing cultural hierarchy relegates the peasantry to a status of permanent inferiority. The little tradition lacks the institutional means for a direct confrontaion with the great tradition. Colonialism further increased the distance between the little and great traditions by diluting ethnic identities.

The Foreword to *Kanthapura* is, again, a criticism not only of the language of the middle class, but also of its ethnic identity and culture which are fragmented. This is characteristic of societies under exploitative colonial regimes. The condition gives rise to social protest. In *Kanthapura*, under the influence of Gandhi, social protest becomes, on the one hand, a movement to reform the inegalitarian Hindu society and, on the other, a movement to end British colonialism. The protest manifests itself as the expression of a critical attitude toward existing institutions and their underlying ethos. Social protest may be initiated by an individual or a community. Individuals, especially charismatic leaders such as Gandhi, play a decisive role in expressing social protest and mobilizing collective support for it.

Space within an Indian village is cut up and allocated to the different castes. Social relationships are interpersonal but hierarchical, with the Brahmin and the pariah at the opposite ends of the spectrum. Into this world steps a young Brahmin, Moorthy, who is educated in the town, and is therefore considered modern. He is a figure of authority because he combines in himself upper-caste status and a college education. He is also a Gandhian, and committed, like Gandhi, to ending British rule as well as ending the inequalities within Indian society such as untouchability and the oppression of women. The Gandhian movement was based on satyagraha, firmness in truth. Gandhi added an ethical dimension to what was basically a social and political movement. The Gandhian bias of the novel is obvious: moral revolution takes precedence over social and political revolutions. It is significant that Moorthy enters the untouchable's house in his own village first before his imprisonment as a revolutionary. While the inspiration of the novel is moral and humanistic, its idiom is spiritual and religious. Stress is laid on such values as righteousness, love, nonviolence, and on ritual beliefs and practices.

Kanthapura is one long, oral tale told in retrospect. There are other tales, interspersed with the main narrative, that begin with the oral tags "Once upon a time," and "This is how it all began," but these are usually digressions. Other characteristics of the oral narrative include the use of songs and prayers, proverbs, mythology, and epic lists and catalogues. The novel is, in fact, unthinkable without the oral tradition. The Foreword itself defines *Kanthapura* as an oral, and not a written, text:

> It may have been told of an evening, when as the dusk falls, and through the sudden quiet, lights leap up in house after house, and stretching her bedding on the veranda, a grandmother might have told you, newcomer, the sad tale of her village. (1963: viii)

It is within the frame of Kannada that the tale is told. English is made to simulate the "thought-movement" and idiom of the old woman, Achakka, who is the narrator. One detects here the notion of linguistic relativity associated with the Sapir-Whorf hypothesis that one's conceptualization of the world is partly the product of the form of the language habitually used to describe it and talk about it. Rao's use of English suggests the appropriation of the structural characteristics of Kannada, as a recent study shows.[17] Consider the opening sentence as an example of syntactic re-creation:

> High on the Ghats is it, high up the steep mountains that face the cool Arabian seas; up the Malabar coast is it, up Mangalore and Puttur and many a centre of cardamom and coffee, rice and sugarcane. (1963: 1)

Janet Powers Gemmill had this translated into Kannada, and again retranslated into English as follows:

> Upon Ghats upon is it, upon steep mountain(s) upon, cool Arabian sea to face making mountain upon, Malabar coast

upon is it, Mangalore, Puttur and many cardamom, coffee, rice, sugarcane centre(s) upon is.[18]

The similarity in the word order is unmistakable, especially the reversal of the word order of subject and verb, and the omission of the verb in the second clause. The deviation is, of course, kept within the bounds of intelligibility. The embedding of the structure of Kannada in English is done with such finesse as to be almost unnoticeable.

Parataxis and simple coordination are syntactic features that generally characterize the oral narrative. They dominate *Kanthapura*. One example will suffice – the celebrated description of the Kartik festival:

> Kartik has come to Kanthapura, sisters – Kartik has come with the glow of lights and the unpressed footsteps of the wandering gods ... and gods walked by lighted streets, blue gods and quiet gods and bright-eyed gods, and even as they walk in transparent flesh the dust gently sinks back to the earth, and many a child in Kanthapura sits late into the night to see the crown of this god and that god, and how many a god has chariots with steeds white as foam and queens so bright that the eyes shut themselves in fear lest they be blinded. (1963: 81)

Idioms are a fertile area for nativization, and here Rao both transplants from Kannada, and implants new ones, eg, "To stitch up one's mouth" (1963: 58), "to tie one's daughter to the neck of" (1963: 35), "a crow-and-sparrow story" (1963: 15) (from "a cock-and-bull story"), and "every squirrel has his day" (1963: 77) (from "every dog has his day").

Adjuncts are frequently used in oral narratives for highlighting a word or phrase, eg, "And the Swami, who is he?" (1963: 41), "... my heart, it beat like a drum" (1963: 182), "She has never failed us, I assure you, our Kenchamma" (1963: 2), and "Our village – Kanthapura is its name" (1963:1).

In an Indian village, relationships are interpersonal. Social stratification is along caste and occupation lines. Idiosyncrasies and physical disabilities often attach themselves as sobriquets to names of individuals. Examples of these abound in the novel: Patel Range Gowda, Pariah Sidda, Post-office Suryanarayana, Husking Rangi, Four-beamed-house Chandrasekharayya, One-eyed Linga, and Waterfall Venkamma.

On ceremonial occasions social relationships are meticulously observed. In a traditional society, certain aspects of conversation are ritualized. Elaborate attention is paid, for example, to modes of address. They reflect the use of language as a means of establishing a friendly rapport between speaker and listener, and of reinforcing communal solidarity. Bronislaw Malinowski refers to this as "phatic communion."[19] For instance, in a host-guest interactional situation, Rao hits upon the exact phrase translated from Kannada to dispel any uneasiness. The guest is coaxed: "Take it Bhattare, only one cup more, just one? Let us not dissatisfy our manes" (21). On the anniversary of a death in a Brahmin family, other Brahmins are invited to a feast, and they are expected to indulge their appetites fully so that the spirits of the dead are pacified. C D Narasimhaiah remarks: "With a people like us, used to being coaxed, the English form, Won't you have a second helping? or the mere Sure you don't care for more? will be ineffective, and even considered discourteous."[20] Culture-sensitive situations like these are not always understood.

Through a choice of strategies, skilfully deployed, Rao has been able to reconstruct the performance-oriented discourse of the traditional oral tales of India. Kanthapura is village India in microcosm – the context that has determined and shaped the expressive devices in the novel.

R̲ao considers his entire work as

> ... an attempt at Puranic re-creation of Indian story-telling: that is to say, the story, as story, is conveyed through a thin thread to which are attached (or which passes through)

many other stories, fables, and philosophical disquisitions,
like a mala (garland).[21]

If Kannada is the prototype for English in *Kanthapura*, Sanskrit it is in *The Serpent and the Rope*. Sanskrit is the obvious choice, as the novel has a strong metaphysical bias. It was in Sanskrit that the philosophical speculations of the Indians found their profoundest expression. Rao's Sanskritic English is not unlike Milton's Latinate English in *Paradise Lost*. The intent is the same: to assimilate into English qualities and features of a prestigious language the writer admires most. As opposed to the Prakrits, vernaculars, Sanskrit was the "perfected" language. The Sanskritization of English should be seen as part of a wider sociocultural phenomenon that has, historically, characterized Indian civilization. Louis Dumont and David Pocock interpret Sanskritization as the "acceptance of a more distinguished or prestigious way of saying the same things."[22] Quotations in the original, together with English translations, from the classical Sanskrit poets, Kalidasa (5th century CE) and Bhavabhuti (7th century CE), and from the devotional hymns of Sankara and Mira, are skilfully woven into the story, and function as a parallel text. Ramaswamy, the protagonist, relapses into Sanskrit to tell his wife Madeleine, as delicately as possible, what he is unable to tell her openly – his feeling of despair as she increasingly withdraws into herself. He finds a parallel in Bhavabhuti's *Uttararamacharita* [The later story of Rama] to which he draws her attention. The occasion has all the solemnity of a ritual, and it represents his farewell to her.

> Ekah samprati nasitapriyatamastamadya ramah katham/
> papah pancavatim vilokayatu va gacchatvasambhavya va//
> Alone, now, after being the cause of the loss of his dear [wife], how should Rama,
> sinful as he is, visit that very same Pancavati, or how pass on regardless of it?[23] (1960: 328)

A powerful recursive device used throughout the novel is the dash (−) to suggest the to-and-fro movement of a thought, its amplitude and density. The dash is used to indicate a break or an interruption in the thought. In between dashes a thought is often insinuated or slipped under the breath, as it were:

> The world is either unreal or real − the serpent or the rope.
> There is no in-between-the-two − and all that's in-between
> is poetry, is sainthood.   (1960: 333)

Philosophical debates are a part of both the Upanishads and Puranas. *The Serpent and the Rope* resembles both. The novel interprets Vedanta in terms of the discourse of fiction. The philosophy is not an interpolation. It is an integral part of the novel, its informing principle.

The philosophical bias is even more pronounced in *The Cat and Shakespeare*. Rao exploits the Vedantic idea of the world being a play (lila) of the Absolute, and the result is an exhilarating comedy in which neither Shakespeare nor his noble language is spared. It is described as "a tale of modern India," and it exhibits none of the communicative strategies of *Kanthapura* or *The Serpent and the Rope*. Unlike the highly individual and expressive idiolects of the earlier novels, that of *The Cat and Shakespeare* is deliberately ordinary, since the intent is to express traditional lore. In this process, Rao has pitted the symmetry of language against the asymmetry of thought with its indirections and paradoxes. The protagonist, Ramakrishna Pai, describes his moment of illumination thus:

> I saw truth not as fact but as ignition. I could walk into fire and be cool, I could sing and be silent, I could hold myself and yet not be there ... I smelled a breath that was of nowhere but rising in my nostrils sank back into me, and found death was at my door. I woke up and found death had passed by, telling me I had no business to be there. Then where was I?[24]

Narasimhaiah has an interesting explanation to offer for the use of the dash in "His heart is so big, it builds a wall lest it run away with everything ... In fact he himself is – running" (1965: 10). He remarks: "And the last sentence is the most deceptive in its simplicity, for the word 'running' after a dash denotes a state of being, not becoming, that is, 'he' and 'running' are interchangeable; running itself is he and he, it."[25]

I suspect Rao's penchant for the finite verb "to be" in both *The Serpent and the Rope* and *The Cat and Shakespeare* has a philosophical basis.

It denotes existence, reality. And since both novels attempt to probe the nature of reality, it is frequently used: "I do not believe that death is" (1960: 9), "So what is real ever is" (1965: 100). The highly reductive style of *The Cat and Shakespeare* is in strong contrast to the expansiveness of the other novels.

The English language does not have sufficiently deep roots in South Asia. It is therefore important for the writer to find his own individual style through which to express his worldview. The reader on his part, if he is not to misread the text, must get to know the writer's epistemological viewpoint or the sum total of beliefs, preconceptions, and values which the writer shares with others within a sociocultural context.

In the course of a visit to India in 1958 to meet Vinobha Bhave, Arthur Koestler made this perceptive observation:

> In Europe the gurus have died out; in India the tradition is still alive, though declining. It was the secret of India's greatness, the emotional yeast by which its great gurus, from Buddha to Gandhi, had kept the race in spiritual fermentation.[26]

The Chessmaster and His Moves offers the most authentic and eloquent account of "spiritual fermentation" in modern fiction that I know of. In appropriating for fiction the domain of metaphysics, Rao has enlarged the possibilities of the genre. The result is a metaphysical novel without equal in our time.

From the earliest times the Indian has shown a special bias for metaphysical speculation about the nature of man and the universe. Long before the rise of Greek thought, he wrestled with the profoundest metaphysical questions. That quintessential Indian text, the Bhagavad Gita, with its roots in the Rigveda and the Upanishads, informs the life of the Indian today as it did in the past. Commentaries on the Gita abound, including those of Sankara and Gandhi, in an attempt to explain its relevance to everyday life. In the Indian tradition, the function of literature was to enlighten – to open our eyes to who we really are.

The Chessmaster and His Moves is firmly rooted in this tradition, which it seeks to illuminate in the form of a novel of epic proportions encompassing on the one hand three worlds – India, France, and England – and on the other, the mind of man. It is the history of man in the twentieth century as he moves from the human to the abhuman to find deliverance from the self in the Self. It is, in fact, structured as a commentary (bhasya) on Indian esoteric knowledge from the Upanishads down, often expressed in the terse, aphoristic style characteristic of that literature. And the principal texts within this tradition of knowledge that are Rao's special concern are those of Advaita Vedanta from Sankara through Atmananda, notably the former's *Brahmasutrabhasya* [Aphorisms on the Brahman: A Commentary], and the latter's *Atmadarshan* [The Perception of the Self, 1946] and *Atma-nirvriti* [Freedom and Felicity in the Self, 1952]. The narrative pattern of *The Chessmaster and His Moves* is indigenous: it derives from the katha tradition of which the finest example is the *Kadambari* of Bana (7th century CE). In the manner of Chinese boxes, the novel collapses a number of stories. Each story provides the context of a situation in which the human drama is enacted. The *Kadambari* connection is explicitly stated on the opening page: "Would you return as parrot, betel vine or bodhisattva? Sometimes I dream of you and call you Kadambari" (1988: 3).

The spirit of Sankara broods over *The Chessmaster and His Moves*. In the Upanishads, also called the Vedanta since they constitute the end of the Vedas, the metaphysical inquiries of the ancient Hindus attain their ripest expression. They raise the question, "Who am I?" (ko aham), and answer it with the statement, "You are That" (tat tvam asi). As an exposition of Upanishadic thought, Sankara formulated his system of Advaita, non-duality. He asserted that only Brahman was real; all else, including the phenomenal world and the sense of individuality, was unreal. They only appeared to be real because of maya, Brahman's power of illusion. When the atman, man's spirit, through meditation and enlightenment, realizes that it is itself of the substance of Brahman and has no separate identity, then it becomes one with Brahman.

As long as man is conscious of the reality of his individual self and of the universe, he cannot but accept his relationships with others and all the objects around him. In this state he lives, works, prays, experiences happiness and pain, and keeps the moral code. However, once he perceives Brahman, all this appears as an illusion. Brahman, then, is the only reality.

The Chessmaster and His Moves contains the statement of an explicit metaphysical position – that of Advaita Vedanta – without making any specific claims for its pre-eminence as compared to other systems of thought. The assertions of Vedanta are regarded as claims to Truth which the reader is expected to behold, not evaluate. Elaborate discourses on metaphysical issues are interspersed with the narrative. Advaita Vedanta provides the focus for both understanding and assessing what happens in the novel.

Man cannot achieve moksa (release, deliverance, liberation) without the knowledge of Brahman. The transcending of mortal existence is his supreme goal. And he reaches it with the help of a guru. "Without a guru, yes, sir, without a guru, you can never reach the end" (537-38).

The Guru and the Disciple

In *The Chessmaster and His Moves*, the guru takes many forms and names: Uddalaka Aruni, Yajnavalkya, Krishna, Buddha, Sankara, Ramana, Atmananda, and Gandhi. Sivarama's own guru is "the great Sage." The guru is the light that illuminates the way for the disciple. It is thus that the traditional wisdom of India has survived into the present through an unbroken succession of teachers. A jivan-mukta (a person endowed with the knowledge of Brahman), the guru can banish the disciple's confusion, and lead him from the unreal to the real, from darkness to light, and from death to immortality. The disciple, again, is enjoined to submit to the four instruments of spiritual knowledge, the sadhanachatustaya: 1. Viveka, discrimination between the real and the unreal; 2. Vairagya, renunciation of desire; 3. Satasampatti, the six treasures (sama, calmness; dama, self-control; uparati, self-settledness; titiksa, forbearance; samadhana, concentration; sraddha, faith); 4. Mumuksutvam, longing for deliverance.

The aspirant begins with the practice of spiritual discipline, yoga. Vedanta favours the discipline of knowledge (jnana-yoga) over those of action (karma-yoga) and love of God (bhakti-yoga). The aspirant follows the path of renunciation and controls his desires. The Upanishads insist on total renunciation of attachment to the world to attain immortality. "When all the desires that dwell in the heart are abandoned, then does the mortal become immortal, and attain Brahman in this body."[27]

The characters in *The Chessmaster and His Moves* may be taken as comprising a scale of being, that is, of spiritual awareness in terms of the ultimate end, deliverance. At the top of this scale is Sivarama. He is followed by those characters who achieve some measure of self-awareness: Ratilal, Michel, Suzanne, and Jayalakshmi.

Sivarama

The metaphysical tone of the novel is introduced by the narrator Sivarama's evaluation of himself: "My mind was essentially metaphysical ... thus evading the human. For, after all, the human has no ultimate significance ..." (1988: 475), and "I too must go my way, my way up some mathematical Arunachala, till I reach the beacon, nirvana. What was it anyway?" (1988: 211). Sivarama is, on his own admission, a seeker after Truth. He offers us the shining example of Ramana Maharshi (1879-1950) who had "come to the end of the Who am I? search" (1988: 211). How did Ramana achieve the end? Elsewhere, Ramana himself provides the answer: "By the inquiry Who am I (nan yar)? The thought Who am I? will destroy all other thoughts and, like the stick used for stirring the burning pyre, it will itself in the end be destroyed. Then, there will arise Self-realization."[28] Though Sivarama has visited Arunachala, he remains as "ignorant" (1988: 211) as ever. Now thirty three years old, he is conscious of his own unworthiness. He describes himself as "lecherous" (1988: 212), "corrupt"(1988: 515), and an "unvirtuous sadhu" (1988: 337). In quest of "the great Sage," he has not rigorously submitted himself to some of the disciplines, especially the renunciation of desire. It is this that still keeps him, an unready disciple, pinned to, and wriggling on, the wheel of birth and death (samsarachakra).

Suzanne

Sivarama's relationship with the four women – Suzanne, Mireille, Jayalakshmi, and Uma – is something of an enigma. Jayalakshmi, the only woman he loves, is already married, and is unwilling to leave her husband Surrendar who is "such a gentle, generous and in some ways noble person ..." (1988: 335). Their love remains unfulfilled. Suzanne and Mireille provide relief, both sexual and emotional, from the torment of love. And with Uma, the sister who adores him, he is neither here nor there. The four women only heighten Sivarama's sense of isolation. Every attempt to relate, sexually or emotionally, only confirms his isolation. Overcome by desire, he is frustrated from performing his dharma, and he seeks deliverance through the intercession of the guru. His search for Truth beyond the human further isolates him.

He is unduly conscious of himself as a Brahmin and euphoric about his Hindu past. His Brahminism is at odds with the way he uses Suzanne and Mireille – they are "substitutes" (126) for Jayalakshmi. All these are obstacles to his becoming a jivan-mukta. Sankara himself speaks of the predicament in a famous hymn, Gurvastakam [Eight Stanzas in Praise of the Guru]:

> Though the lore of the Vedas takes up its dwelling on your tongue,
> Though you be learned in scripture, gifted in composing prose and verse,
> Yet if your mind is not absorbed in the guru's lotus feet,
> Of what use are they to you? Of what use, indeed, are they?[29]

Sivarama, who refers to his guru as "the great Sage" along with Sankara, Ramanuja, and Madhava, is as yet not totally absorbed in his guru's lotus feet.

His relationship with both Suzanne and Mireille bear out his unflattering assessment of himself. Suzanne loves and adores him, but he is incapable of loving her. To him she is only a "big loaf of bread – french bread. It smelt rich, and a little garlicy, and ready for being taken" (1988: 163). It is difficult to reconcile Sivarama's spiritual hunger with his appetite for women (Remember Padu's description of him? "He is a vampire. He eats women's flesh" [1988: 163]).

In Book One of the novel, there is the movement of the male (purusa) toward the female (prakriti), of Sivarama toward Suzanne and vice versa. One's movement toward one's sexual opposite, seeking union, has symbolically an unconscious meaning. The sexual act does, at the unconscious level, attempt to erase the duality of the masculine and feminine principles. Sexual union has the implication for the unconscious of rebirth, and through rebirth of nirvana. This is the conclusion Sivarama comes to after lying with Suzanne on his return from visiting Jayalakshmi in London. "Every man who unites with his woman anoints himself a king. Thus I was reborn. Blessed, blessed Suzanne!" (1988: 190). Suzanne, of course, expects Sivarama to marry her, though she is uncertain about him. He is throughout indecisive about marrying her, and she eventually leaves him. Why doesn't he marry her? Sivarama too asks this question of himself, and attempts an explanation: "Why didn't I marry S is a question that cannot be answered. There are some questions that have no answer" (1988: 3). Perhaps an explanation is to be sought in what he tells Jayalakshmi: "One marries only once ... And one marries always a virgin" (1988: 555). A statement such as this could be misconstrued, and Sivarama accused of being a cad. But then Sivarama, as he tells the Rani Saheba, has "little respect for what people call morality" (1988: 690). His failing remains with him to the end, raising serious doubts in us about his preparedness for the spiritual discipline essential to be a jivan-mukta.

A Shaiva Brahmin from Chidambaram, Tamil Nadu, Sivarama Sastri is a mathematician and a "disciple of Ramanujan" (1988: 128) in whose shadow he works at the Institut International de Mathimatique Pure in Paris. The study of numbers for its own sake has a long and honourable tradition in India. That Indians had a clear conception of the abstract number is evident from the work of Aryabhata (5th century CE), the earliest writer on algebra, Varahamihira (6th century CE), Brahmagupta (7th century CE), Mahavira (9th century CE), and Bhaskara II (12th century CE). They fully understood the mathematical implications of zero (sunya) and infinity. Srinivasa Ramanujan (1887-1920) is, of course, a distinguished heir to this tradition.

It is an exciting time in the history of Indo-French relations. Andre Malraux visits Nehru as an emissary of de Gaulle. In 1962, France had withdrawn from Algeria, and this had provided de Gaulle with the opportunity to play a more vigorous international role. It is during the heyday of the Fifth Republic that Sivarama arrives from Calcutta as a research scholar. While in Calcutta, he had met Jayalakshmi, daughter of the Maharaja of Vilaspur, and wife of Raja Surrendar Singh. At one level, the novel charts the course of their ill-fated love whose deeper resonances are plumbed by Rao by invoking Indo-European myths and legends.

Jayalakshmi

In the West, the most impressive representation of love as passion (Eros, kama), as opposed to love as compassion (Agape, karuna), is to be found in the legend of Tristan and Iseult which celebrates the rite of love in which the individual is torn out of himself and opened to an awareness of himself that is transcendental. As told by Joseph Bedier (1864-1938), it is a "tale most sad and pitiful to all who love." For Tristan and Iseult the Fair are reunited only in death. This is the *amour courtois* (courtly love) of the troubadours of Southern France of the high Middle Ages. The lover idealizes his beloved, and she occupies an exalted position over him. His feelings for her ennoble him. Her beauty makes him long for union with her as a means of transcending himself. It is a paradox that the love as presented by the troubadours is extramarital and illicit, and at the same time ennobling. Their ideal of love prohibited sexual intercourse between the lovers. This prohibition had the effect of investing any contact or gesture with immense erotic significance. Jayalakshmi, for instance, acknowledges that Sivarama breathed life into her, lit her up when, one Diwali day in Vilaspur, he touched her navel (1988: 159-60). In its religious praise of the eternal feminine, the chansos of the troubadours reflect elements of the worship of the Virgin Mary. In *The Chessmaster and His Moves*, the Tristan legend is deployed repeatedly as a universal myth to illuminate the love of Sivarama and Jayalakshmi. In this quadrangular relationship, Suzanne and Mireille are represented as Iseult Blanchemain, Iseult of the White Hands. Mireille and Jayalakshmi have returned from a visit to Chartres. While having tea at Mireille's, Jayalakshmi calls Sivarama who thinks of the Tristan legend during the conversation: "... Mireille must have (and unconsciously) compared herself to Iseult Blanchemain. The black sail would, anyway, pass by in a moment – the other Iseult, then, is truly dead. Would Tristan stay with Blanchemain then?" (1988: 554).

Of the many Hindu myths that resonate throughout the novel, perhaps the most potent is that of Krishna and Radha. Their relationship epitomizes the highest form of love – passionate, illicit love; for Radha is another man's (the cowherd Ayanaghosa's) wife. Krishna plays his flute at night in the forest of Vrindavan. At the sound of his enchanting music, wives leave their husbands' bedsides for the forest, and dance all night in ecstasy with Krishna. In the rapture of love, one is transported beyond temporal laws and relationships. Radha is usually depicted in Sanskrit poetics as a parakiya, she who is another's, a woman married to someone other than her lover. Rukmini, the princess of Vidarbha, on the other hand, is a svakiya, she who is one's own, Krishna's principal wife. Radha as a parakiya stresses the revolutionary otherness of the world to which Krishna's flute beckons. By responding to its call, women leave conventional morality behind to revel illicitly with Krishna, their lover. The Bengali Vaisnava poet, Chandidas (15th century CE), expresses Radha's archetypal situation thus:

> What god is that
> Who moulded me a woman?
> I am always alone
> Being married and watched.
> Since falling in love
> Is a disgrace for me,
> I must then kill
> My meaningless life.
> I am not free
> To open my mouth
> But I am in rapture
> With another man.[30]

The Radha-Krishna myth serves as a profound symbol of man's longing for the ultimate reality, and functions as a subtext, throwing light on the complexity of love between Sivarama and Jayalakshmi. On one of their last evenings together, in Sivarama's apartment on the Avenue de Bretuil, Jayalakshmi sings a song of Mira (1498?-1547), the Rajasthani devotional poet whose work is a distillation of the Radha-Krishna myth:

> Mere to girdhara gopala dusara na koi
> tat mat bhrat bandhu apno na koi. (1988: 565)
> Only Gopala, holding up the mountain, have I. There is no other.
> I have no father, mother, brother, friend whom I can call my own. (1988: 717)

Jayalakshmi discovers her voice in the rough-hewn but poignant speech of Mira.

And Jayalakshmi's departure for India at the end of the novel movingly reenacts a familiar Hindu ritual. The scene is Orly Airport, Paris:

> And under the huge clock, in the middle of the hall, she made me stand, and covering her head (and before the whole far away world), she touched my booted feet with both her hands, long, very long, and rose touching back her eyes. I felt so unworthy, I lifted her up.
> "O Jaya," I almost shouted, "never, never do such a thing."
> "I wish you could be king!" And a lone tear ran down her left eye.
> I shivered. My body understood. My mind a straight bamboo of fire.
> "I must leave now. The turk awaits me." And she walked intent towards the exit. So, that was it, the story (1988: 706).

In some Vaisnava traditions, Krishna subordinates himself to Radha by touching her feet to acknowledge his devotion to her. This reverses the usual form. By touching Radha's feet, Krishna becomes her devotee. Jayalakshmi, on the other hand, true to form, touches Sivarama's feet, likewise acknowledging her devotion and love. Already enthroned in her heart as king, she wishes he could exercise total sovereignty over her. However, that is not to be, for both know that "For a Hindu woman there is but one marriage" (1988: 335), and "One marries only once ... And one marries always a virgin" (1988: 555). Jayalakshmi remains, like Radha, a parakiya to the end. Again, like Radha, she has reached her man through love. She is now truly and forever home. But Sivarama, in his search for Truth, remains forever homeless.

Thus the novel conflates two potent and resonant myths, from two ends of the Indo-European world, in an attempt to understand precisely the relationship of passion to compassion. The Buddha is usually invoked as the exemplary figure in this context. Prince Siddhartha renounces his home and the world, and becomes the Compassionate One. The moral is not entirely lost on Sivarama as is evident when he narrates to Jayalakshmi at London Bridge Hospital the renunciation of Gautama: "All one needs is the swordlike sincerity of Gautama. How far I am from that, Jaya" (1988: 126).

Myths are, of course, of the substance of our psyche, and they put us in touch with ourselves. They awaken us to a new awareness of the meaning of life and of reality itself. It is through myths that we enter into contact with our own deepest self and with other human beings. Above all, they invite us to a spiritual awareness far beyond the realm of subject and object.

At another level, the novel enacts the conflict between desire (kama) and duty (dharma), that is, between the force of passion and the pressure of self-control. This is aesthetically expressed in the relationship of the erotic (sringara rasa) to the compassionate mood (karuna rasa). The novel makes its impact on us not through the conflicts of individuals, but through the timeless conflict between desire and duty. Rao's aesthetic is rooted in the scheme of the purusarthas, the four aims of human life (duty, wealth, desire, and liberation) that Hindus consider to be the essence of Hinduism, and which help to reconcile life's possibilities. The conflict is changed into aesthetic experience by Rao's presentation of his characters' responses to different situations. It may, thus, be argued that the characters are not individuals but universal types within social contexts that reflect the hierarchical nature of traditional Indian society. If we accept this reading, Sivarama and Jayalakshmi could be seen as vehicles for exposing the inner tensions in that society. This explains Rao's practice of loading every rift with mythological ore: Krishna and Radha, Shiva and Parvati, Rama and Sita, Satyavan and Savitri. These myths are held up as paradigms that function as signposts or paths to guide the characters in their uneasy passage through this world. We have seen how forcefully the Radha-Krishna myth speaks to us in making explicit the relationship of Sivarama and Jayalakshmi. Their passions behind them, their hearts are stilled into repose by an ancient ritual. That is the mood in which we find ourselves at the end of the novel, a mood that calls us out of ourselves to a transcendental realization of unity.

Michel

It is in his encounters with Michel and Ratilal that Sivarama offers the most explicit statement of his metaphysical position. Michel, a linguist at the Centre National de la Recherche Scientifique, is a Hasidic Jew and a survivor of Birkenau who makes a passionate apology for the Jews' right to live in honour, and not as the world's untouchables. Hasidism, as a protestant movement within orthodox Judaism, has much in common with devotional Hinduism (bhakti), especially in its emphasis on the importance of the inner service of God rather than the observance of ritual laws. The single most important aspect of this service is devekut (cleaving to God in joy). Hasidism gave new value to the life of the ordinary Jew who could not aspire to any great understanding of Jewish lore. "Put a Brahmin and a Rabbi in the same room," Rao once said, "and a major work of philosophy can reasonably be expected."[31] Michel presents an overview of the persecution of Jews from its beginnings in Egypt under Pharaoh Rameses II (1304-1237

BCE) through the destruction of Jerusalem in 586 BCE by the Babylonian king Nebuchadnezzar II (630?-562 BCE) to the nightmare of the Holocaust in our own time. The Jews, he remarks, "were never meant for war ... We were made for books – for the Book and the Torah" (1988: 645). And, again, speaking in a combative tone, he tells Sivarama: "You indians – indian thought as such – since the eighteenth century – have usurped our place. We were the priests of the western world" (1988: 659), evidently referring to the inroads that Indian thought had made in Europe in the late eighteenth century. The true Gandhians, he continues, were the Jews of Poland as they "went to their death in prayer" (1988: 666). Book Three of the novel explores the reasons for the Holocaust, and attempts to expiate it and all human suffering. Sivarama informs Michel that the real dialogue in the world is not between the East and the West, but between the Brahmin and the Rabbi (1988: 226). The discussion then turns to Brahman, and how we may know him. Michel asks Sivarama:

> "But do you know Brahman?"
> "No. Not yet! For to know Brahman really, one has to become Brahman, to become It."
> "Yes, It," he smiled, as if he'd found a new idea to play with.
> "But," I warned, "from Him to It is the direct mortal leap – the truest death of death."
> "How accomplish then, this 'goat' leap?"
> "Through Him that is It," I said slowly, awkwardly, and for some reason my hair stood on end, and I shivered (1988: 671).

Sivarama here paraphrases a famous verse from the Mundaka Upanishad: "sa yo ha vai tat paramam brahma veda brahmaiva bhavati, "[32] ("He who knows that supreme Brahman becomes Brahman himself.") The Upanishad emphatically states that only the renouncer (sanyasin), who has given up everything, can know Brahman. Sivarama tells Michel that one knows Brahman, It, only through the guru, Him. The premonition of his own unknown guru puts him in a state of deep, calm fever. The guru, thus, is the Chessmaster, and His moves, the compassion and the grace that wipe away the disciple's ignorance.

Ratilal

A successful Jain businessman in Paris, Ratilal is on the verge of renouncing the world and becoming the disciple of a guru in India when Sivarama meets him. Like the Buddhists, the Jains were seriously dedicated to the quest for moksa. They lived as ascetics, devoting their entire lives to the task. Jainism denies the authority of the Vedas and the orthodox traditions of Hinduism. We are told that Ratilal was "well versed in philosophical dialectics, both indian and european ...," and his "search seemed personal and fundamental" (1988: 525). On the death of his wife Satyavati, he takes the vow of celibacy. Less of an intellectual than Sivarama, Ratilal appears to be better prepared for the practice of spiritual discipline. Also, his claims for his metaphysical position are modest: "Until I go to the end of my path, how can I know, how can anybody know, if these teachings answer the questions we ask, or they do not?" (1988: 548). That, I believe, ought to be the tone and spirit in which to conduct philosophical inquiries. The dialogue with Ratilal presents a third alternative, besides Vedanta and Buddhism, to moksa. This speaks eloquently for Rao's openness to alternative systems of thought, though all of them have one and the same goal – moksa.

What *The Chessmaster and His Moves* ultimately presents is a vision of Indian civilization from its radiant origins in mythology as Jambudvipa, the Land of the Rose-Apple Tree, to Gandhi's New India. One facet of that vision we are privileged to witness is the splendour of Benaras, Hinduism's fabled city. Rao invokes it in a breathless ritual:

> ... and after a holy bath in the river, going towards the Vishvanath temple, white in clothes, with coconut and fruits, incense and camphor in hand, holding a copper pot of the pure Ganga water, you await, till you come to the silent

crowded temple, and then you hear the mantra being spoke, the bells going off behind and above you, and you throw your sacred water on the head of the linga, bathed in sandalpaste, marigold flowers, and pilgrim-waters, the temple cows outside munching their very long green grass.
(1988: 350-51)

We are invited to savour its rasa, the richness and plenitude of its spirit, and come away refreshed, whole. Herein, perhaps, lies the "secret of India's greatness" that so discriminating a visitor as Koestler was able to observe.

Notes

An earlier version of this essay was presented at an international symposium, "*Word as Mantra: The Art of Raja Rao*," at the Center for Asian Studies, University of Texas at Austin, USA, on 24 March, 1997.

1. Raja Rao. *The Policeman and the Rose: Stories*. Three Crowns Books. Delhi: Oxford UP, 1978. xiv.
2. Raja Rao. *The Chessmaster and His Moves*. New Delhi: Vision Books, 1988. Subsequent citations from this edition are indicated in the text parenthetically by page number.
3. R Parthasarathy. "The Future World Is Being Made in America: An Interview with Raja Rao." *Span* (September 1977): 30.
4. Braj B Kachru. *The Indianization of English: The English Language in India*. Delhi: Oxford UP, 1983.
5. Raja Rao. *Kanthapura*. London: Allen and Unwin, 1938. Rpt New York: New Directions, 1963. vii. Subsequent citations from the American edition are indicated in the text parenthetically by page number.
6. Raja Rao. *The Serpent and the Rope*. London: John Murray, 1960. 330. Subsequent citations from this edition are indicated in the text parenthetically by page number.
7. I have not been able to trace the source of this quotation.
8. *Chandogya Upanishad*, VI.8.7. *The Principal Upanishads*. Ed & trans S Radhakrishnan. London: Allen and Unwin, 1953. 458. Subsequent citations from the Upanishads are from this edition.
9. Patanjali. *Vyakarana Mahabhasya*. Ed F Kielhorn and Rev K V Abhyankar. 3rd ed 3 vols. Pune: Bhandarkar Oriental Research Institute, 1962-72. 3: 58.

10. Bhartrhari. *Vakyapadiya, with the vritti and the paddhati of Vriabhadeva*. Ed K A Subramania Iyer. *Kanda* 1. Deccan College Monograph Ser 32. Pune: Deccan College Postgraduate and Research Institute, 1966. 201.
11. Louis Renou. *Études védiques et paninéennes*, 17 fasc Paris: Institute de civilisation Indienne, de l'Université de Paris, 1955-69. 1-12.
12. Raja Rao. "The Writer and Word." *The Literary Criterion* 7.1 (Winter 1965): 231.
13. Qtd in André Padoux. *Vac: The Concept of the Word in Selected Hindu Tantras*. Trans Jacques Gontier. SUNY Series in the Shaiva Traditions of Kashmir. Albany: State U of New York P, 1990. 373-74.
14. Padoux. *Vac* 374.
15. Arthur A Cohen. *Osip Emilievich Mandelstam: An Essay in Antiphon*. Ann Arbor: Ardis, 1974. 42.
16. R Redfield. *Peasant Society and Culture: An Anthropological Approach to Civilization*. U of Chicago P, 1956. 67-104.
17. Janet Gemmill. "The Transcreation of Spoken Kannada in Raja Rao's *Kanthapura*." *Literature East and West* 18. 2-4 (1974).
18. ibid 194.
19. Bronislaw Malinowski. "The Problem of Meaning in Primitive Languages." *The Meaning of Meaning*. Ed C K Ogden and I A Richards. New York: Harcourt Brace, 1923. 315.
20. C D Narasimhaiah. "Indian Writing in English: An Introduction." *The Journal of Commonwealth Literature* 5 (1968): 14.
21. M K Naik. *Raja Rao*. Twayne World Authors Series. New York: Twayne, 1972. 103.
22. Louis Dumont and David Pocock, eds. *Contributions to Indian Sociology* 3. The Hague: Mouton, 1959.
23. Bhavabhuti. *The Later Story of Rama [Uttararamacharita]*. Part 1: Introduction and Translation by Shripad Krishna Belvalkar. Harvard Oriental Ser 21. Cambridge, MA: Harvard UP, 1915. 39.
24. Raja Rao. *The Cat and Shakespeare*. New York: Macmillan, 1965. 113-14. Subsequent citations from this edition are indicated in the text parenthetically by page number.
25. C D Narasimhaiah. *Raja Rao*. Indian Writers Series. New Delhi: Arnold-Heinemann India, 1975. 163.
26. Arthur Koestler. *The Lotus and the Robot*. New York: Macmillan, 1961. 23.
27. *Brahadaranyaka Upanishad*, IV.4.7. *The Principal Upanishads*. Ed and trans Radhakrishnan. 273.

28. Ramana Maharshi. *The Spiritual Teaching of Ramana Maharshi.* Boulder, CO: Shambhala, 1972. 6.
29. Sankara. *Gurvastakam* [Eight Stanzas in Praise of the Guru]. *Atmabodhah* [Self-Knowledge]. Trans Swami Nikhilananda. Madras: Sri Ramakrishna Math, 1967. 232.
30. Chandidas. *Love Songs of Chandidas: The Rebel Poet-Priest of Bengal.* Trans Deben Bhattacharya. New York: Grove Press, 1970. 76.
31. Qtd in M V Kamath. "The Brahmin and the Rabbi." *The Illustrated Weekly of India* (24 August 1980): 47.
32. *Mundaka Upanishad*, III.2.9. *The Principal Upanishads.* Ed and trans Radhakrishnan. 691.

ROBERT D KING

RAJA RAO, TEACHER

I would like to be completely nameless, and just be that reality which is beyond all of us – Raja Rao.

"Teacher" is perhaps the first word that comes to mind when one thinks of Raja Rao. "Novelist" yes, "philosophical novelist" even better, and though "scholarly Sanskritist" (Salman Rushdie's peculiar description in *The New Yorker*) is not right, it is not altogether wrong either. But it is as teacher that I know Raja Rao best, and it is of that side of him that I choose to write.

I had first thought to write of Raja Rao and France, where he spent so many years and half-years even after Austin, Texas, had long become his home of record. A title for an essay had already suggested itself: "West Toward Home: Raja Rao and France." But I found that the picture would not come into focus – Raja Rao and France, France as Raja Rao's notional home: not India, not America, but France. It did not work. "[T]he earth didn't want it, ... they didn't want it, they said in their hundred voices, No, not yet, and the sky said, No, not there." The thoughts came to me to be named and written like objects as they came to Rilke; but in Rao language, silence would not become the common word or light.[1] The pictures were there in the mind, so clear at times, so far away at others; but they would not become words. The words were like a flock of frightened geese, circling in the distance, uncertain, afraid to land.

No matter where my point of entry – Malraux (Raja Rao's *semblable, – son frere*), Denis de Rougemont, the stern, rocky Catharist redoubts of southern France, Rama and Madeleine of *The Serpent and the Rope* – I kept returning to Texas, to Austin, to Raja Rao and the University of Texas, to the apartment on Pearl Street, to my own experience of Raja Rao, to my conversations with him. I always came back to what I had learnt – "absorbed" is the apter word – from him over all these years about India and spirituality and life's deeper content; to how all that knowledge and perception I had learnt from Raja had settled in me, in my comprehension and occupancy of life; had come to rest in the courses on India that I teach and the books on India that I write; of how much a part of me Raja's *Weltanschauung* had become. And, beyond me, I thought of that generation of Texas students who experienced Raja Rao in the classroom, whose teacher he was in the 1960s and 1970s and whose lives were never the same again.[2]

Robert Graves tells us ("To Juan at the Winter Solstice") that

> There is one story and one story only
> That will prove worth your telling,
> Whether as learned bard or gifted child;

For me, writing here about Raja Rao, that one story, the only one that will prove worth my telling, is the personal one – my Gangetic pilgrimage, with Raja Rao as guide.

Which is how my subject became not Raja Rao and France but Raja Rao, Teacher – *My* Teacher, actually – starting on one path, finishing on another altogether different. I came to the University of Texas as a young Professor of German and Linguistics in 1965, and Raja began his formal affiliation with the University as a member of the Faculty of Philosophy in 1966. I did not know him personally then, or for a long time afterward–

though he was a campus icon, acclaimed for his lectures on Buddhism and Eastern thought. But by the 1980s I did know him as a friend, and my real education on India began (though I had gone there first in 1963 and felt that I knew at least a few things about the country).

Raja Rao would deny that he is a teacher, and above all that he is a guru.[3] No, above all not a guru. He shuns those designations. But there he is wrong. He is a teacher, a guru, and a generation of his Texas students are the witnesses. As I am too. His method is subtle, seductive, humorous at times. I do not think Raja Rao is aware of whether he is talking to a class or to many people or to only one person. It is always a subdued discourse, a monologue at times, quiet, level, steady. I construct no theory of his teaching – I sometimes feel that all theory for Raja Rao is adharmic – but examples of the Rao technique will do to show his method.

No Vedantic concept is harder for the American mind, or more generally the Western mind, to grasp in its fullness, than dharma. Maya and karma, they are problematic, yes, but they can be explicated – translated using little English words; their meanings can be sorted out. We know "illusion" and "action, the law of consequences." We can comprehend, whether we agree or not, that a single lifetime might be insufficient either to reward a man for his conduct or punish him for his misconduct hence rebirth and all the rest. Our thought-world accommodates maya and karma without great strain, whether we believe in them in the Indian sense or not.

Dharma is at a higher semantic altitude. I recognized the first time I knew the word that what we were dealing with here was the Middle High German word *reht*;[4] which at first seems bizarre (what on earth could India and medieval Germany have in common?) but makes more sense than it seems, because both societies – the ancient Indian (Mauryan or more especially the Guptan) and the courtly society of medieval Germany – were remarkably similar in many ways.[5] Caste would not have been unfamiliar to Parzifal – or to European courtly society as a whole. In both India and Europe social stratification was rigid; class boundaries were absolute and behaviour absolutely prescribed except in dissonant epics such as Gottfried von Strassburg's *Tristan*.[6] Guptan culture saw the emergence of Kalidasa and the Puranas, the "flowering of classical Sanskrit literature."[7] Middle High German culture produced Wolfram von Eschenbach, Walther von der Vogelweide, and the great courtly epics of Hartmann von Aue, Heinrich von Morungen, and Reinmar von Hagenau.[8]

Martin Joos's description of medieval West European culture during its *Blutezeit* ("time of flowering") carries over to Guptan culture with only trifling modifications:

> Rarely if ever in the history of life and letters have the members of a society ... so narrowed their field of interest – and so thoroughly integrated what they allowed to be within it. The result is like a formal garden: it covers a small area; inside it, no growth is tolerated which cannot be harmonized by rule with the rest ...; and all that lies outside is forgotten while one is within it – and can be forgotten, for no outside thing need be taken into account to explain what is within.[9]

According to Joos, *reht*, in Middle High German (we are speaking here of *circa* the twelfth century, give or take a few hundred years), meant:

> (1) the essential quality of a person, (2) his natural status, (3) the sum of his rights and duties, or any one of them, (4) the network of social structure, (5) "law" in general, and (6) "justice, correctness." ... Each animal and each thing had its own *reht*, by virtue of which it necessarily played its part in the economy of the universe.[10]

Compare Joos's summation of the submeanings of *reht* with what the great Indologist J A B van Buitenen wrote about dharma.

> Dharma, in Hinduism, is the cosmically or "religiously" determined activity of all existing beings to maintain the normal order in the world ... These activities called dharma are imposed as a kind of natural law on all existent beings

> in the universe ... It is the dharma of the sun to shine, of the pole to be fixed, of the rivers to flow, of the cow to yield milk, of the *brahmin* to officiate, of the *kshatriya* to rule, of the *vaishya* to farm.[11]

Dharma, van Buitenen teaches us, "is the observance of the necessary acts that keep the world intact."[12] *Reht* in other words: medieval man would have recognized it immediately.

But how to convey that, and all that lies behind it, to a class of American students to whom the medieval thought-world is more foreign than the Tibetan *Book of the Dead* or the Hebrew cabbala? It is no easy task; there is no simple way. Is it even possible? The usual translations of dharma mean nothing, less than nothing, in the West and have not in a hundred years. The literal translation "law" says too little, "moral obligation" or "moral duty" too much.[13] Does one dare to say that dharma is that which holds the world together?[14] Does that help an American student comprehend dharma? Certainly not.

Raja Rao pointed the way for me by a phrase, an *apercu*, which he used once giving a guest lecture in a class of mine on India when answering, for surely the thousandth time, the question what is dharma: "Dharma is the umbilical cord to the Absolute." Reflect on the enormity of that! Every content word in that identity carries equal weight: "umbilical" – primal and essential; "cord" – the link, the sacred thread; "Absolute" – the End of Man, moksa. A stunning way of putting it. And ever since, I have had less trouble teaching my students dharma. I do not begin with his dramatic formulation but that is where I end, and it works, sometimes. I always caution my best students, the ones who want to know more than I can teach them: Do not rush it, give it time. Understanding, in one view, begins with the renunciation of the desire to understand.

As a second example of the Raja Rao method, take Delhi. It was my good fortune to have first learnt India in the mofussil, not the great cities. Unlike most Westerners, who do not know the mofussil, my experience of India began in the tribal outback of Orissa and ended only a long time later in Delhi and Agra and Mumbai. To me India has always remained what I knew it as at first: red earth, green leaves, Indian crows with the characteristic little white shawls around their shoulders, roads only a bullock cart could traverse, a railway line snaking through village India of the Eastern Ghats like a finger of the hand of God. It was like Kurtz' river, taking me back to a compressed centre of essentiality. I have never loved Delhi as I have, let us say, Calcutta or Bhubaneshwar or Khajuraho, and why is this? I once asked it of Raja Rao, during a tiny intermission in an evening of talk. And he gave the answer immediately: "Delhi is not an Indian city; it is a Persian city." (Had he reflected on that? Had he ever said it before? Is that why Delhi and North India generally play little, if any, role in any Raja Rao story or novel?)

The point can be argued, I suppose, but one has only to see in the mind's eye a Khajuraho or a Lingaraj in Bhubaneshwar, or the Surya temple of Konarak on the Bay of Bengal, magnificent in black ruin, with their distinctive Hindu temple architecture and pervasive spirituality, juxtaposed alongside a Delhi or an Agra to appreciate the depth to which Persian forms permeated Northern India and made it forever different and alien. Sir Edwin Lutyens, oddly enough, caught the native idiom better in the Rashtrapati Bhavan. I have the fugitive impression sometimes when I am there that the older parts of Delhi and Agra are Persian cities from which "Persians" have temporarily withdrawn or been expelled as after a war (as Partition was a war; and like most wars neither an end or a beginning: merely a failure). It is the same impression one forms in Polish cities like Wroclaw and Poznan, once Breslau and Posen, where to the "Persians" correspond the Germans, expelled from these long-German cities at the end of World War II. Such places are Polish now in every regard – in language and law and customs and all else; but they look German with their *Fachwerk* houses and neat farms, their flowers in the window sills. In something like this sense an Agra or Old Delhi, the Delhi of the Red Fort and the Jama Masjid, "looks" Persian, "feels" Persian. If the Urdu language of the rabbit-warren Muslim streets of Old

Delhi could be reified, then it would be a graceful statue dappled with Persian graffiti. Such was the linguistic and architectural legacy of the great Mughals.

I could never have thought that way, much less written any of that, if Raja Rao had not pointed out the way to me with his succinct summation dropped casually in the middle of a much longer conversation. "Delhi is not an Indian city; it is a Persian city." An *apercu* that lingered in the mind long after and eventually spread its roots.

So many times I have heard students ask Raja Rao: "How do I become Hindu?" Even wise men cannot agree on this one – or whether the thing is even possible (if one is a Westerner), which I doubt – but his answer has never varied when I have been there to hear it, and it is this: "It is not your dharma to become Hindu – I myself am not Hindu, I am Vedantist. It is your dharma to be a Westerner who understands India and loves it well. Become that. Forget this nonsense about becoming a Hindu."[15] Which comes, though I did not know it then, from the Gita (18, 47):[16]

> Better to do one's own duty imperfectly
> than to do another man's well;
> doing action intrinsic to his being,
> a man avoids guilt.

I have myself never been seriously tempted to "become" anything that I am not, nor was shaped by my culture and birth to be. But if I had been, that dictum of Raja Rao's would have been a barrier I should never have been able to pass. My dharma, as much as any man can know it, is to be an American who studies India and Indian ways; to be a student of India. And to pass on what I have learned to my students.

A supreme lesson drummed into a generation of Texans by Raja Rao is the corrosive evil of dualism – body versus mind, body versus soul, wisdom versus experience. All is seamless continuum: Tat tvam asi. In the very first letter he wrote to Ivar Ivask, editor of *World Literature Today*, upon hearing the news that he had been selected for the 1988 Neustadt Prize, Raja Rao wrote:

> I write this letter to you, at the hour of dusk, the auspicious hour, because it is non-dual, and therefore transcendent: the moment when the day and night do not meet, but leave a depth of silence, and so the edge of sound, lingering towards its origins. It's a noble hour because it affirms the unnameable.[17]

Above all what we, his students, his chelas, have learned is that India is nothing if it is not spiritual. Recall the dialogue from that astonishing early scene in *A Passage to India*, when Mrs Moore has entered the abandoned mosque where Dr Aziz is: "Madam! Madam! Madam!" He tells her that she has no right there, that she should have taken off her shoes (which in fact she had done); and she asks whether (since she *had* removed her shoes) that did not mean that she was allowed? "Of course, but so few ladies (memsahibs) take the trouble, especially if thinking no one is there to see." And Mrs Moore says: "That makes no difference. God is here."[18]

"God is here." At which point – David Lean's direction of Victor Banerjee (Aziz) makes more of this moment than does the book, correctly I think – the world changes in an instant; the words have disturbed the universe. Aziz's face softens, he accepts Mrs Moore, their differences fade, it is the beginning of love. "God is here." India is spiritual, that first, last, always.

The apotheosis of this, for me, came in 1985 when we held at the University of Texas a conference on "India in the Year 2000". I was the Liberal Arts Dean in those days, and I had invested much besides money in a successful conference on India. The ordinary instruments all agreed that the conference, which had been a part of the the Government of India's Festival of India, had been very successful. We had a sterling array of participants: political scientists, natural scientists, economists, sociologists, geographers. We had the best minds of both India and America. All had important things to say.

Raja Rao attended the conference. He asked not a question the first day. That, I knew meant that he was not happy with what was going on around him. I perceived the rumbles of the dormant volcano. On day two of the conference, the volcano erupted. Having listened without posing a single question to the wise men, the economists, the sociologists, the linguists, all the clever bodies, for two days, he rose, almost shaking with anger, to say: "What country is this you have been talking about? I do not recognize it. I do not know it. Where is spirit, where is love, where is dharma? You cannot speak of India without using these words. You have betrayed India by speaking of it as if it were any country." And we all sat — those of us attuned to Raja Rao's discontent — chastened, embarrassed, hateful of our science. India is nothing if it is not spiritual, that is the lesson of Raja Rao.

Let me end my Gangetic pilgrimage in a place — sacred geography is after all the essence of India — which I visited in December, 1996: the Anantisvara temple in Chidambaram not far off the Bay of Bengal in Tamil Nadu, south of Chennai. I had long-deferred reasons for wanting to visit this ancient temple, one of which had everything to do with Raja Rao the language lover, absorbed in words and Sanskrit.[19] Patanjali, the author of the classical grammar *Mahabhasya*, has traditionally been identified with Patanjali, the philosopher and yogi who wrote the Yogasutra, the celebrated treatise setting out the eight limbs from which all schools of yoga are derived. We do not know for certain whether Patanjali the Sanskrit grammarian was also Patanjali the philosopher, so fused in the folk mind have the two become, but we do know that the Patanjali — or the two Patanjalis — to whom the *Mahabhasya* and the Yogasutra are attributed is traditionally represented as a demigod: a coiled snake from the waist down and depicted sometimes with a cobra-like hood composed of five serpents over his head.[20]

That is why I originally wanted to go there, to Chidambaram — to visit this shrine consecrated to the demi-deity linguist-cum-philosopher Patanjali. It was the pilgrimage of a quondam linguist in search of more substantial nourishment than formal theory. And that as it turned out was as satisfactory an experience as I had wanted it to be, experiencing this reification of linguistics in ancient India as the centre of the intellectual enterprise, religiously sanctioned, its practitioners philosopher-priests. But the visit became more than a stop on a linguist's homage to a shrine of his discipline's past. At the very centre of this ancient Shaivite temple, behind the statue of the dancing Shiva, the Nataraja, there is a room. The priests who tend the temple call this room "The Secret of Chidambaram." It is empty. The priests say it has always been kept empty in order to teach a lesson, which is that the spiritual experience we all seek as we work our way through life is nowhere to be found but in our own heart. Not in statues and carvings and representations of the gods, not in material possessions, not in good works, but in the richness of emptiness, the emptiness of a bare room.

Raja Rao's lesson, though I could not absorb it whole at any one time, has always been that we must each of us seek our way to salvation in our own way. It is a lonely search, not communal; each man is alone. Out of our emptiness will come knowledge, understanding, forgiveness – all that matters. There is only the One Way: not Indian, not Western, but both. Never the dualistic Either-Or; always the monistic Both-And. The secrets lie in our own hearts.

> This knowledge I have taught
> is more arcane than any mystery –
> consider it completely,
> then act as you choose. (Gita [18, 63])[21]

His message, I have now come to know, is not so much knowledge and understanding as it is something very close to the supreme achievement of love. Or perhaps it is simply love.[22]

That, in the end, is what we all learnt from Raja Rao, Our Teacher. We learnt love. That is our debt, a debt that can never be repaid in full but only in karmic instalments, of which this is one.

Notes

1. Something that Raja Rao wrote in his acceptance of the Neustadt Prize in 1988 had affected me greatly when I first read it, and often since: "The writer or the poet is he who seeks back the common word to its origin of silence, in order that the manifested word become light. There was a great poet of the West, the Austrian poet Rainer Maria Rilke. He said objects come to you to be named."

2. A steady note in Raja Rao's discourse is the decline of the search for values during his time in America: "In the '60s and the '70s the search for values was very remarkable. I was really thinking America would be the greatest nation ... [But] most of modern literature is psychological. There is no search in it. Philosophy began to go down in '78 and '79." (Interview with Anne Morris, *Austin American-Statesman*, 23 March 1997.)

3. "I am not a guru," Rao said. "A guru is pure consciousness, a person with no ego." He laughs. "I have an ego. Yes. Still!" (Interview with Anne Morris cited previously).

4. The dictionary meaning of both Sanskrit dharma and Middle High German *reht* lies in the intersection of Law-Right-Justice.

5. I first began to reflect on this during my first stay in India, in the summer of 1963, when as a graduate student I worked in a remote tribal area of southeast Orissa (District Koraput) on the Remo (or Bondo) language of the Munda language family. The life of these tribal people has changed very little in hundreds of years. What struck me most forcibly at the time – I was more involved in medieval studies than linguistic – was how all activity was communal, collective, anonymous. There was no room for the outsider, the loner, any more than there had been in the courtly society of medieval western Europe.

6. "Dissonant" because Tristan and Isolde cheated not only Isolde's husband Marke but betrayed virtually all of the medieval courtly ideals, most notably *maze* "moderation," *maze* being among the highest of the medieval virtues. The theme is developed most extensively in Denis de Rougemont's classic *L'amour et l' occident*, translated as *Love in the Western World* (New York: Harcourt, Brace, 1940). De Rougemont's point is that Gottfried was a Cathar, a mystic, a heretic; "love" therefore for Gottfried was *eros*, not *agape*. I once wrote an article on this: "*Triuwe* in Gottfried's *Tristan*," *Canadian Journal of Linguistics* 17 (1972), 159-66. I showed that the Middle High German word *Triuwe* which one normally translates as "fidelity" (cf Modern German *Treu*) meant in *Tristan* (but no other courtly epic) something more akin to "passion" or "intense, physical love" *eros*.

7. Hermann Kulke and Dietmar Rothermund. *A History of India*. Calcutta: Rupa & Co, 1991. 91.
8. And, not to lose the thread to Raja Rao, recall that it was this European medieval culture in its Southern French variant that drew the young Raja Rao over the dark waters: "And Ramaswamy [Raja Rao's *Doppelgänger*] takes the way of active life – a student of history who goes to France for research in Albigensian heresy (the Catharist heresy, ruthlessly stamped out by orthodoxy), of connecting the Cathars with the Vedic ancestors, marries a Frenchwoman (older than him) who teaches history and is interested in tracing the origin of the Holy Grail in the Cathars." From C D Narasimhaiah, *The Swan and the Eagle*. Simla: Indian Institute of Advanced Study, 1969. 166.
9. Martin Joos and Frederick R Whitesell, *Middle High German Courtly Reader*. Madison, Wisconsin: U of Wisconsin P, 1958. 237. Alberuni made a remarkably similar observation about Hindu society in the tenth century when he wrote concerning caste (varna): "All institutions of this kind are like a pedigree, as long as their origin is remembered; but when once their origin has been forgotten, they become, as it were, the stable property of the whole nation ... And forgetting is the necessary result of any long period of time, of a long succession of centuries and generations." See *Alberuni's India*, ed Ainslie Embree. New York: W W Norton & Co, 1971. 100.
10. Joos and Whitesell, 238.
11. "Dharma and Moksha," in *Studies in Indian Literature and Philosophy*, ed Ludo Rocher. Delhi: Motilal Banarsidas, 1988. 114. (Reprinted from *Philosophy East and West* (1957): 33-40.
12. ibid.
13. What does "moral" mean in a world where values seem threatened with extinction? (*"Il faut supposer Sisyphe heureux."*)
14. "Do I dare/Disturb the universe? ... And how should I then presume?/And how should I begin?" (T S Eliot, "The Love Song of J Alfred Prufrock".)
15. Raja Rao's teaching methods do not include the suffering of fools gladly.
16. In the translation of Barbara Stoler Miller, *The Bhagavad Gita*. New York: Bantam Books, 1986. 149.
17. Ivar Ivask, "Introduction," *World Literature Today*, 62.4 (1988): 526.
18. *A Passage to India*. 17-8.
19. "After all, I was born on the Temple street of Chidambaram, where not even a cur barked. Remember a loud noise was inauspicious for Brahman purity, and even dust settled quickly into sanctuary silences." From Raja Rao, *Comrade Kirillov*.

Delhi: Orient Paperbooks, 1976. 27. (The "I" in the quotation is not Raja Rao but another of his *Doppelgängers*. Raja Rao was born in the town of Hassan in what then was Mysore State.)
20. J F Staal, *A Reader on the Sanskrit Grammarians*. Cambridge, Massachusetts: MIT P, 1972. xvi.
21. Miller, 152.
22. "Love" as *agape*, not *eros*.

C D NARASIMHAIAH

RAJA RAO: EACH WORK
A MAGIC CASEMENT

"Magic Casement," as is well known, is Keats' term – Keats, that "one complete artist" of his age, whose every poem is fed on the magic of myths. Surprisingly, so is every human being in India – poet and peasant, prince as well as pauper. Analyze the chemistry of their being, and you will find the mythological component most pronounced. Even a fact of history is not borne in on an Indian unless it is mythologized. Hence, the Western accusation that Indians have no sense of history. Ironically, some of the better historians in the West today tend to look at "history as myth" in a bid to enhance its value, while for a public man like Jawaharlal Nehru even myth becomes history. Obsessed with the "temper of science," – the result of his scientific training at Cambridge and earlier – he begins his *Discovery of India* with characteristic impatience, wanting to "clear the cobwebs" of the past and give his country a "garb of modernity," but is soon overwhelmed by the intermingling of myth and legend in drab, everyday life – a sturdy peasant or a beautiful woman walking in the countryside often reminds him of the frescoes of Ajanta and he wonders "how the type has endured amidst the horror of poverty and misery" only to reprimand himself: "Who am I to break" the chain of "continuity and vitality of the past?" As Prime Minister, he goes to address an Irrigation Engineers' Conference at a dam construction across the Ganga, and asks the engineers if they have told the workers the story of the Ganga because it is the story of Indian Civilization; on its banks great empires once flourished and when they decayed, new ones took their place. He realizes that it is not the engineers' business, but if approached imaginatively "the stone and the water they work with will acquire a new dimension" and they would feel "lifted from the drudgery of their daily existence."

Which brings me to my present concern, for that is how Raja Rao's novel *The Serpent and the Rope* affected me when I first read it – I began to feel my ancestors in me. Even the aborigines of Australia today claim that they hear their ancestors advise them in their "dreamtime," "not to seek to create a new world but to try and fit into the old world." All this before I ever met Raja Rao or even knew anything about him or his writing. And I wrote an enthusiastic piece on *The Serpent and the Rope* in my mendicant journal, *The Literary Criterion*, when R K Narayan, our more widely known novelist, told me privately how thrilled he was by this phrase or that turn of thought in the novel and, unasked, spoke to his friend, the editor of India's most influential periodical, *The Illustrated Weekly of India*, to seek a contribution from me on this new novel. To my surprise the editor even printed a shorter version of my *Criterion* essay and did so without any editorial maltreatment.

Narayan's graciousness reminded me of Ezra Pound's classic utterance on the publication of T S Eliot's *The Waste Land*: "It is time we shut our shops." However, it was not an instant success – today's spurious reputations are a recent phenomenon, thanks to the scandalous collusion of Publisher and Media: advances of fabulous sums of money to the author have become a criterion of literary excellence. The reader's response counts for nothing; it just doesn't come into the picture. I have in mind Vikram Seth's 1400 page door-stopper, *A Suitable Boy*, which is said to have sold 400,000 copies. *The Serpent and the Rope* took at least three years before it became a topic of conversation among academics and was mentioned in influential circles. Slowly, it began to be recognized as an authentic literary masterpiece from India.

It was then that some of Raja Rao's admirers first heard of his earlier publication, *Kanthapura*, written when he was twenty six. The Foreword, of a page and a half, by the author struck some of us as being the literary counterpart of announcements of the first epoch-making invention or discovery in science by a youthful prodigy, destined to blaze a trail across the world. Strangely, this book of village life and the troublesome Gandhian movement was published by a prestigious English firm, Allen and Unwin, and later reissued by Oxford University Press; not, let it be said, in response to huge sales, but as an incentive to other universities, on its getting a college prescription from my university.

Meanwhile, it became a target of attack for Indian academics decrying its "Indian English," then a pejorative term for its numerous departures from Standard English. I remember a mere undergraduate at a conference in Jamaica, who called the bluff when a British linguist described what he considered "deviations from Standard English" in West Indian English. The young man vehemently asserted, "The English I speak and write here is standard to me." But the last Englishman was still to be found in India! Even men in public life sought to be custodians of "Chaste English" and both found hospitable columns in a widely circulated provincial English newspaper in Bangalore. *The Daily* carried on its agitation against Raja Rao until he was honoured with the Padma Bhushan by the President of India. Then bold letters on the front page proclaimed that the "author of the controversial *Kanthapura*" had received the coveted honour. Those who had ridiculed him returned to sing his praises.

Meanwhile, *Kanthapura* had built up a stable base amongst undergraduates, most of whom hailed from villages and small towns. And they responded spontaneously to the Foreword which spoke of every village having a sthalapurana, the legend of the place, of a god or godlike hero and heroine. It touched a chord in their hearts, as Jane Austen's *Pride and Prejudice* did not. As they turned the first page they were startled to find an invocation to Kenchamma, the goddess of the village, chanted in the language of international recognition, as if it was the vedic mantra uttered by our Aryan forefathers as they poured into the Gangetic Valley. Its folk rhythms had been miraculously infused into English while they had been told by T S Eliot that the rhythms of modern poetry were conditioned by the internal combustion engine:

> Kenchamma, Kenchamma Goddess
> benign and bounteous
> Mother of Earth, blood of life
> Harvest Queen, rain crowned
> Kenchamma, Kenchamma

Here was the tempo of Indian life so effortlessly infused into English as "the good breath of the ballad" had been transferred into formal Australian poetry. Here in India, says Raja Rao,

> It was the sage Tripura who made penances to bring her down to the Earth and she waged a battle and fought the demon that the blood soaked and soaked into the earth and that is why Kenchamma Hill is red. Thank heaven, not only did she slay the demon but she settled down among us and has never failed us in our grief. If rains come not you fall at her feet and say, our fields are full of younglings and you have given us no water. Tell us Kenchamma, why do you make our stomachs burn? And Kenchamma, through the darkness of the sanctum opens her eyes wide and she smiles a smile which you have never beheld.

You see in this fragment of a paragraph not only myth but "social transactions" rendered authentic in terms of art by the villagers' patois, their sing-song syntax, what the Australian poet Les Murray called "Boetian strain" as against the mainstream Athenian which English Romanticism was to him. In much the same way that Dante made great poetry out of "vulgar tongue" in preference to learned Latin; or Ignatio Silone, who went back to his boyhood dialect of Fontamara, abandoning the Italian he learnt at school. I bring in Ignatio Silone because he acted as a catalyst to Raja Rao in the writing of *Kanthapura*. The name Kanthapura itself has grown out of "Kantha," meaning romantic wife in Sanskrit poetry, but, tested in the fire of Gandhi's movement, transformed into Kasipura in the end, the other name for holy Benaras. This is a tribute to the novelist's celebration of the Feminine Principle.

The tale came nearer to their bosoms as the villagers began to claim Corner-house Moorthy as "Our Gandhi." Peasant and Pariah, unmarried girls and childless widows, college boys and their orthodox Brahmin parents, Nine-beamed-house Range Gowda and Pariah Rachanna, Waterfall Venkamma and Bent-legged Chandrayya and Fig House and Front House People – all rallied round him in the consecration of a linga, God Siva's phallic stone symbol, which the boys unearthed and started the celebration of birthdays of this god or that saint – the Indian calendar is dotted with festivals every other day. It is by appealing to this time-tested faith that Gandhi built up support against British rule – a voluntary mass movement as conveyed in the novel in claims like "Let the first be mine and the second mine, insisted Venkateshia."

If purists see in these expressions what they call "departures from Standard English," I should ask them to read what Henry James wrote to Conrad, who was not born to English: "I read you," said James, "as I listen to great music, with the deepest depths of surrender." The English that Raja Rao's characters speak here has its correspondence in the contours of thought, feeling and sensibility which couldn't fail to make an immediate impression on people.

That is how Gandhi affected his countrymen and touched the deepest springs of their being. Aldous Huxley who wrote a critical essay, "Where Gandhi Failed to See," nevertheless concluded by conceding that a politician who eats a good dinner makes a poor leader in India – Huxley registered an entire tradition and summed up a whole people's response to Gandhi in saying what he did. Here is the foremost leader of a National Movement who fixes a day for his agitation against the British but on Hitler's bombing of St. Paul's Cathedral, withdraws it, because, "I can't make England's difficulty my opportunity."

As a result of police excesses the people of Kanthapura went through untold suffering – Rangamma's house lost its roof, Nanjamma's house had all but fallen, others had their doors broken. Range Gowda who was "a tiger" to the authorities had become lean as an areca. The village was half deserted. "There's neither man nor mosquito," is the novelist's summing up. But it should not be forgotten that out of it all, as in the Easter Rising of Ireland in 1916, "a terrible beauty is born." What could the people of Skeffington Coffee Estate run by the Red man show by way of compensation in moral and spiritual terms?

The tragedy that struck Kanthapura and other such places elsewhere in the country added up to Gandhi's spirited call for the British to quit India – Quit India became a vigorous movement. And though not known at large, Gandhi's words on suffering as the law of life served as an epigraph to *Happy Valley*, the first novel of Patrick White, Australia's lone Nobel Laureate, and his dozen subsequent books enacted the theme of suffering in its different variations.

Did Professor Hardgrave hear distant echoes of it all when his invitation to me opened with a singular reference to *Kanthapura* which "would be 60 years old next year"? I wonder if even Professor Hardgrave realized that in thinking of honouring an Indian in America, he was heir to his own country's legacy displayed in that great, though short-lived, movement called Transcendentalism in the beginning of the last century, thanks to the confluence of French and German idealism, Indian antiquity, and Sufi mysticism infused into native American eclecticism. Emerson called his wife "Mine Asia" and affirmed that the story of Nala and Damayanti was of greater import to him than the morning's newspaper. Thoreau, his follower, shouted in annoyance, "what kind of life do we live in Massachusetts? There's no festival, no procession, no ceremony?"

Indeed, for him, "one verse from the Bhagavad Gita is worth the whole State of Massachusetts put together." And a less-known member of the group, Ellery Channing, one day decided to close his law office and open a school with the exhortation, "Let the next generation be my clients."

Here in our midst is a novelist whose second novel *The Serpent and the Rope* saw its publication almost a quarter of a century after he wrote *Kanthapura*. So exacting are his demands on creativity – in the manner of our great sculptors and weavers of the legendary textile called muslin, India's pride and the world's envy. Did he say with Keats, "I would sooner fail than not be with the great"? For I don't know of another novelist in India, in English or our other languages, who has absorbed the best traditions of India and Europe even as Aurobindo did in his poetry and literary criticism, and Coomaraswamy in art history. He has packed a wide range of experience into making it a truly international novel. The novelist sends his central character to France, a country which becomes his by right of vision; he marries a French woman and worships her gods, for to wed a woman is to wed her god, and gives his inner sanction to the sentiment that all roads in Paris lead to the Notre Dame. He participates in his French wife's rituals, ceremonies and superstitions, for he feels liberated enough to accept the other's as his own – all inclusion, they say, is a sign of culture, all exclusion is want of it. He endears himself to Madeleine's family. But she keeps drifting from one thing to another, from Brahminism to Buddhism to Tantric worship, without letting her heart throb in compassion – indeed the channels of her bloodstream must be blocked when she asks Ramaswamy, "Why did you come?" And she, a Buddhist, speaks of some stupid spot which she can call her own and sends word to Ramaswamy that he would do well to seek divorce, for that is the Law, whereas for Ramaswamy "Law is the death of Truth."

It can well be argued that Raja Rao, in writing an autobiographical novel, identified himself with Ramaswamy and isn't detached enough in looking at Madeleine. Well, all we can do in respect of works of art is seek corroboration from disinterested readers, who in this case may be non-Hindu, non-Buddhist, asking them what they feel about the novelist's disposition toward Madeleine, for Raja Rao is exploring profound issues here, that concern modern man in that they explore how far one's religion or country can liberate or inhibit one to conduct oneself as befits a man of culture, indeed as befits a decent human being. He is in the line of the Brahmin priests who invited the Charvakas, materialists, to preach Godlessness from the precincts of their temples.

When Ramaswamy's marriage breaks down it would have been easy for Savithri and him to come together, but the novelist is detached enough to send Ramaswamy to his guru and Savithri to stump Pratap – both in keeping with their Dharma. The opposites evaporate, from what Keats calls "their relation to Beauty and Truth" for example King Lear. The appreciation of difference is the basis of true culture – if it can work in a political set-up, it is surprising that it should entail endless labouring in human relationships.

Here, too, is a novelist who makes it possible for a betel-chewing non-Brahmin, Govindan Nair, to teach Brahman to Brahmins. In the previous novel, the very second sentence in the opening paragraph expresses a qualification about his belonging: "Brahmin is one who is devoted to truth and all that," the ironical "and all that" making for endless reservations, enacted in the course of the novel. It is Nair more than the Brahmin characters in the novel, who has a true apprehension of life here and life beyond, as testified by the ease with which he crosses the wall of illusion; it is he again who brings in a Pariah animal, the cat, to show them the way to Truth, because the question is "Have you ever seen a Kitten fall?" "Trust to the Mother Cat, then." What an enviable apprehension and how incisively presented!

These three novels, therefore, represent to me the highest point in Raja Rao's creative endeavours. Which means that I confess to a reservation about his last novel, *The Chessmaster*, for some his crowning achievement. Crowning, I admit, in his perception of Reality or what Coomaraswamy calls "percept of the concept." But I fear I must admit to a reservation in respect of its enactment as a work of art, the way the material organizes itself as the novel's texture, that is, in the manner that the novelist makes his apprehensions comprehensible – the latter being the privilege of the art form. Does Art preclude a vision of the Beatitude? Perhaps it is the difficulty of keeping a balance between the demands of philosophy and of art, that made T S Eliot once complain of the increasing secularization of the English novel, and D H Lawrence fear that Fiction and Philosophy had for long fallen out, like a haranging couple.

In any case, let me hasten to add that you can't judge Raja Rao's total achievement from what I or someone else thinks of his last work – that would be like judging Shakespeare's monumental and diverse output by his last play *The Tempest*; that is to amputate his body of work, not judge it. In Raja Rao's case even two short stories like "Javni" and "Nimka" stand out as the work of a great master who demands mention in the same breath as Tolstoy and Dostoevsky and who forbids easy generalization. Speaking for myself, he poses a challenge to a critic of literature and the very business of criticism: which is to keep alive our interest in a serious work and make us return to it again and again, and not presume to say the last word – the Indian tradition of neti, neti, not this, not this, had better be our guide.

BRAJ B KACHRU

RAJA RAO:
MADHYAMA AND MANTRA

Introduction[1]

This paper contextualizes Raja Rao's *Kanthapura*, published in 1938, within what is now the canon of Indian English creativity. In fact, Rao's *Kanthapura* provided a liberating mantra in the formative years of Indian writing in English. This sixtieth anniversary of its publication, therefore, is an appropriate occasion to place that mantra in a broader historical context and to study its emancipating impact on creativity in English in South Asia and beyond. In 1937 [published in 1938], Rao said, about writing in English, that "the telling has not been easy" since "one has to convey in a language that is not one's own the spirit that is one's own" (vii).[2] This dilemma is between madhyama, the medium, and mantra, the message – the channel and what it conveys. The medium represents "an alien language" and yet, Rao adds, English is "not really an alien language".

This explanation, and its elaboration, is articulated in the "Author's Foreword" to *Kanthapura* (vii-viii) of less than 500 words – just 461, to be exact. It is these 461 words that I would like to discuss and contextualize here. In retrospect, sixty years later, one can argue that this Foreword as a mantra envisions an emerging canon, and circles the possible boundaries of its canonicity – linguistic and contextual. The Foreword outlined an agenda and became Rao's own credo of creativity: indeed, it proved the trailblazer of what turned out to be a liberating tradition in world Englishes. It was, as Parthasarathy rightly says (1987: 157), "revolutionary in its declaration of independence from English literature."

A number of sentences from this Foreword have repeatedly been quoted, analyzed, and paraphrased, both in Rao's India and in other parts of the world, where creativity in English has gradually become an integral part of the national literatures. And, as time passed, with various modifications and interpretations, the credo acquired almost the status of a manifesto in founding what, in the '80s, has been called "liberation linguistics."[3] Rao, of course, did not use the term "liberation"; he did not need to. Instead, he just carved a different path consistent with his native tradition – that of convergence, cohesion, and assimilation. What he did by this mantra, and later, was to put around the English language the Brahminical "sacred thread," thus initiating English into India's linguistic family. It is in this subtle and suggestive way that Rao performed the samskara ("initiation rite") and brought the English language within the mainstream of India's linguistic and cultural tradition (parampara).

In this sense, then, Rao's credo was both a reinvention of the language, and a reconstruction of how it could be defined. In his reconstruction, Rao recognized the implications of three basic features of the induction of English in India's pluralistic context: the bilingual's creativity, the formal and functional hybridity of the language, and the recontextualization of a colonial linguistic weapon within the age-old assimilative linguistic history of India.

The Caste of English

In 1937 Rao talked of an Indian identity of English – he was presenting a vision and expressing a kamana – an intense desire. This visionary insight was, however, elaborated further over twenty years later, in 1978. In a short paper appropriately titled "The Caste of English," Rao attributes a varna, a caste, to the language. He actually blends his metaphysical and pragmatic visions concerning English, and places the language on the same elevated pedestal of Truth as the one on which Sanskrit ("The Perfected Language") has traditionally been placed by the Brahmins, as devavani ("divine or heavenly language"). And Rao adds a pragmatic aspect to the language by saying, "so long as the English language is universal, it will always remain Indian":

> Truth, said a great Indian sage, is not the monopoly of the Sanskrit language. Truth can use any language, and the more universal, the better it is. If metaphysics is India's primary contribution to world civilization, as we believe it is, then must she use the most universal language for her to be universal ... And so long as the English language is universal, it will always remain Indian ...

It is this type of mantra which Rao uses to respond to the ideological and linguistic war which Thomas B Macaulay (1800 – 1891) had launched over a century earlier, aiming at the soul and mind of India.

Rao is also responding to India's linguistic chauvinism, particularly that of the post 1960s, when he says:

> It would then be correct to say as long as we are Indian – that is, not nationalists, but truly Indians of the Indian psyche – we shall have the English language with us and amongst us, and not as a guest or friend, but as one of our own, of our caste, our creed, our sect and of our tradition.

By incorporating the language within the caste, within the creed, and within the sect, the samskara is complete – and for Rao the Indian identity of English is complete. The initiation, the samskara, has "liberated" both the medium and the message that the medium conveys. And now, truly, "the Empire talks back," reciting its own mantra in multiple voices.

The mantra is not just incantation, the intoning and chanting of a word or a phrase. It is more than that. It is a medium of thought, and

> ... it is not the conceptual, discursive, differentiating form of thought (vikalpa) that accompanies empirical language. This is more intense, more effective thought, a thought that is also one-pointed since it is connected with a concentrated form of speech, endowed with special potency and efficacy.
> (Padoux 1990: 373)

This explanation of mantra is consistent with what has been labeled the "Kashmirian theory of mantras."[4]

Anatomy of the Mantra

What Rao's mantra regarding English does is to contextualize English within five refreshingly new perspectives.

First, there is a reference to language as medium and as a vehicle of a message. The medium, as mentioned above, is "not one's own." But the spirit that the medium conveys "is one's own."

The identity is with the functions and acculturation that the language has acquired in Rao's India – the form or substance appropriately Indianized to serve these ends.[5]

The second perspective concerns the daunting issues of reconciling local culture and "thought-movement" in an "alien" language ("... thought-movement that looks maltreated in an alien language.")

And here Rao is encountering the Whorfian dilemma. But having said this, Rao pauses, and almost as an after-thought, he reconsiders his use of the distance-marking term "alien". In reconsidering the "alienness" of English, and how it becomes "Indian," Rao says:

> I used the word "alien," yet English is not really an alien language to us. It is the language of our intellectual make-up. We are all *instinctively bilingual*, many of us writing in our own language and in English [emphasis added].

The term "instinctively bilingual" has immense implications for our understanding of the multilingual's language behaviour. This concept of "instinctive" bilingualism has yet to be understood in societies where monolingualism continues to be treated as a normal linguistic phenomenon and multilingualism is viewed as linguistic aberration. And this latter view continues to be held in many linguistic and educational circles in the West.

I don't think that the concept of "instinctive bilingualism," or at least some inherent human capacity for multilingualism, has even now entered the theoretical conceptualization in explaining bilinguals' strategies (see, eg, Kachru 1987, 1996 a and b, and 1997). Consider the relatively recently articulated views of social scientist Shills and linguist Crystal. Shills (1988: 560) claims that:

> The national language of literary creation is almost always the *language of the author's original nationality*, there are, of course, exceptions, such as Conrad, and, at a lower level Nabokov and Koestler, Apollonaire and Julien Green. But for writing about public or political matters, a foreign language is often used effectively [emphasis added].

When asked to explain the difference between people who have native speaker awareness of a language and those who do not, Crystal's response is rather mystifying. He says (cited in Paikeday 1985: 66-67) that it is quite unclear what to make of cases like Nabokov and the others. George Steiner *(Extraterritorial Papers)* talks about them as having no native language. But these are marginal cases.

And, elaborating on who is a "native speaker" (of English), Crystal continues (68):

> I know several foreigners whose command of English I could not fault, but they themselves deny they are native speakers. When pressed on this point, they draw attention to ... their lack of childhood associations, their limited passive knowledge of varieties, the fact that there are some topics

which they are more "comfortable" discussing in their first
language. "I couldn't make love in English," said one man
to me.

These views only partially reflect the contexts of creativity and proficiency across speech communities, and are particularly inadequate when considering language use in the multilingual societies around the world.[6]

Rao's third perspective relates to hybridity in terms of the convergence of visions when the English language is used in pluralistic contexts:

> We cannot write like the English. We should not. We cannot write only as Indians. We have grown to look at the large world as part of us.

What is called the Rushdiesque language, and defined as "a hybrid form of post-colonial and post-modern narrative discourses" by Langeland (1996: 16) has its well-conceptualized beginning in Rao. Langeland considers this aspect of Rushdie's technique (1996:16)

> ... as a radical linguistic operation implanting new cultural impulses into hitherto more narrowly ethnocentric language.

This was the point that Rao was addressing a decade before Salman Rushdie was born and over a generation before Rushdie's *Midnight's Children* (1981) was published.

Fourth, Rao recognized that there is a linguistic consequence of this convergence that results in formal distinctiveness of the Indian variety of English. He compared the situation with Irish and American English, both of which had to undergo a long struggle for what may be called their "linguistic liberation":

> Our method of expression therefore has to be a dialect which will someday prove to be as distinctive and colourful as the Irish or the American.

Fifth, hybridity results in stylistic transcreation, and here again, Rao refers to American and Irish varieties of English:

> After language the next problem is that of style. The tempo of Indian life must be infused into our English expression, even as the tempo of American or Irish life has gone into the making of others.

Thus, Rao sees that the "tempo of Indian life" must be "infused" in our literary creativity. That "tempo" is well represented, as Rao reminds us, in our literary parampara, in our epics, and in the Puranas – in "high" culture and the "vernacular" culture:

> And our paths are interminable. The Mahabharata has 214,778 verses and the Ramayana 48,000. The Puranas are endless and innumerable.

And what are our conventions of discourse? What is our "culture of grammar?"

> We have neither punctuation nor the treacherous "ats" and "ons" to bother us – we tell one interminable tale. Episode follows episode, and when our thoughts stop our breath stops, and we move to another thought. This was and is the ordinary style of storytelling.

In these five points Rao provides a context and broad features for the Indianization of the English language. In other words, he outlines the grammar of discourse, and emphasizes the culture that the language was gradually acquiring in India.

These five perspectives, then, encapsulate the foundations of what one sees now as the emerging canons of English in its second diaspora— the Asian and African diaspora. This mantra authenticates the crossover of English in its altered sociocultural contexts.

The five perspectives may be summarized as:

1. The relationship between the medium (madhyama) and the message (mantra).

2. Reconceptualization of the contextual appropriateness of English

as a medium of creativity.

3. The relevance of hybridity and creative vision and innovation.

4. The relevance of language variety, linguistic appropriateness, and identity.

5. Stylistic transcreation, cultural discourse, and their relationship with local parampara.

The text of *Kanthapura* that follows the Foreword actually gives life to Rao's vision of creativity, and he tells us that "I have tried to follow it myself in this story"(viii). He takes up his own challenge to demonstrate that the "thought-movement" is not "maltreated in an alien language." And in his use of English, he makes a distinction between two linguistic functions – *intellectual* and *emotional*:

> It is the language of our intellectual make-up – like Sanskrit or Persian was before – but not of our emotional make-up. We are all instinctively bilingual, many of us writing in our own language and in English.

In Rao's novel – his sthalapurana – a new linguistic tradition, a new dimension of creativity in world Englishes began to develop in the 1940s. This experimentation in creativity in English was not restricted to India. We witness various versions of such gradual – and sometimes subdued – experimentation in West Africa, in East Africa, and in Southeast Asia and the Philippines. The new paradigm for the use of the colonial language was unfolding itself, primarily with local initiatives. The earlier conceptual frameworks were being altered and set aside, and fresh initiatives were being outlined.

The credo of 1938 became the cornerstone for what followed in the years to come. In different ways, and with different emphases, we hear these new voices in, for example, Nigeria's Amos Tutuola, Chinua Achebe, Buchi Emecheta, and Wole Soyinka; in Kenya's Ngugi wa Thiong'o; in Somalian Nuruddin Farah; and in Rao's own contemporaries in the Indian subcontinent, particularly in the stylistic and thematic experimentation of post-1947 writers such as Upamanyu Chatterjee,

Amitav Ghosh, Mukul Kesavan, Rohinton Mistry, Arundhati Roy, I Allan Sealy, Vikram Seth, and Shashi Tharoor.

In 1982, Rushdie tells us that "we can't simply use the language [English] in the way the British did: it needs remaking for our own purposes."[7] The next generation had taken Rao's mantra and now the parampara continues.

When Rao emphasizes the term *Indian* with English, for him English is a part of the region's multilingual linguistic repertoire. And his modifier *Indian* with English is not to be understood in the sense in which it was being used in Rao's time by, for example, Goffin (1934), Kindersley (1938), and earlier by Whitworth (1907). These scholars, as I have discussed earlier (eg, Kachru 1993, 1991), viewed Indian English primarily within the "language deficiency" paradigms, and Whitworth (1907: 6) considered Indian innovations "linguistic flights, which jar upon the ear of the native Englishman." The use of the term Indian English is also not identical to what poet Nissim Ezekiel has labeled his "Indian English poems."

Rao's creativity goes back six decades; these have been years of innovation and stylistic experimentation for him. *Kanthapura* provides the first conceptualization of Rao's view of "Indian" English, and this conceptualization continues to evolve in other distinct ways in his later writing. Parthasarathy (1987: 160) insightfully explains such experimentation as "ritually de-Anglicized English." The use of *ritually* with *de-Anglicised* is significant here.

> In *Kanthapura* English is thick with the agglutinants of Kannada; in *The Serpent and the Rope* the Indo-European kinship between English and Sanskrit is creatively exploited; and in *The Cat and Shakespeare* (1965), English is made to approximate the rhythm of Sanskrit chants. At the apex of this linguistic pyramid is ... *The Chessmaster and His Moves*, wherein Rao has perfected his experiments with the English language spanning more than fifty years.

What we see, then, is that each of Rao's novels in its distinct way authenticates and expands one or more aspects of Rao's 1938 credo. And each stylistic experiment appropriates, as it were, the English language on Indian terms. The Indian canon of English gains yet more energy, vitality and identity. In other words, it legitimizes itself in India's sociocultural context. The works that followed *Kanthapura* are essentially Indian in their contextualization, their multilinguality, their linguistic and cultural hybridity, and to use Thumboo's term, in linguistic and cultural "crossover."

Let me give just one example of the code-mixed texture of Rao's discourse here. Linguistic hybridity is skilfully foregrounded in *The Chessmaster and His Moves* (1988). The novel brings together eight languages: three Western (English, French, and Greek), and five Indian (Sanskrit, Tamil, Hindi, Hindustani, and Urdu). Witness the following:

> "Ca va?" answers Jayalakshmi, adjusting her necklace.
> "Est-ce qu'on va le trouver aujourd'hui," he continues, the last word said with such heaviness.
> "Si le Seigneur le veut."
> "Mais quel seigneur?"
> "Lui," she said with a mischievous smile, as if thinking of someone far away, very far away.
> "Qui donc?"
> "Son Altesse le lion." Of course she was speaking a lie.
> "Le tigre?"
> "Non," she said, and turned to her father, asking if the mail had come (195).

And Rao with equal ease switches to Hindi:

"Maji kahan gaye hain? Achlia. Suno. Vo kab arahi hai? – Agaye? Kapada badalke arahi hai? Achha. Padu. Bye-bye" (175).

In designing the text, in incorporating language into the stream of narrative, "instinctive biliguality" is taken for granted. There is no concession made for monolingualism. And no textual clues are available for comprehension of Sanskrit, French, or Hindi. The burden of linguistic and cultural intelligibility and interpretation is on the reader. Consider, for example, sentences such as:

> "Our alaya, the true home, is forever the Himalaya." (46)
> "It is all prarabdha, it's written on our foreheads." (49)
> "For either you touch suffering, and so suffer, or reach to the other side, and be it. One is kashta and the other duhkha." (84)
> "A brahmin should not touch jhoota, especially, my jhoota." (130)
> "And so you and your beads, and the sorrow. Duhkha me duhkha milaja." (108)

The "mixing" and "switching" play distinctive stylistic and identity roles in his writing and they are much more marked in *The Chessmaster and His Moves* than in the earlier *The Serpent and the Rope* (1960). In the former, the glossary includes 336 words, as opposed to just 27 in the latter.

One linguistic device that contributes to what has been termed Rao's metaphysical style is his aphoristic use of language. One is tempted to say that in such use the medium is English, but the underlying thought-process is almost Vedantic. Rao is adept in the process of transcreation from Sanskrit. Note the following examples,

> "To be is to is-to-be nowhere." (48)
> "To be is to know, but to know is rarely to be." (63)
> "Going in non-going." (55)
> "Not to be is truly to be." (95)
> "Death's death is what death seeks." (104)
> "To belong you must be lost." (143)
> "The essence essences essence." (162)

If *Kanthapura* was his first specimen of the implementation of his credo, the conceptualization of *Indian* English, the full range of such experimentation is found in his later works.

In his lexicalization from India's languages, Rao follows a somewhat different path than his contemporaries Mulk Raj Anand, Khushwant Singh, and Ahmad Ali. It is not just lexical foregrounding, but it is part of discoursal cohesion – an integral part of the style. The incorporation of Sanskrit words is one device that Rao uses for the metaphysical and Vedantic contextualization of the narrative. This type of Sanskritization of discourse results in the linguistic dilemma of establishing translation equivalence between Sanskrit and English. What Rao does is to include in the stream of narrative *semantic* sets of the following types:

Adi Sesha, "The Primal Serpent"; Advaita, "nondual"; ahamkara, "I-ness"; ahanta, "emphasis on personal I"; agnana, "ignorance"; anaman, "nameless"; bhavati, "becoming"; dhih, "intellect"; ka, "light"; prana, "life-breath"; samsara, "cyclic becoming or existence"; satvic, "pure"; tapas, "austerity"; and yoga chakra, "the subtle nervous system."

Structure as the Puranic Form

In his structural conceptualization of the text, Rao again looks back to the tradition, to the parampara of sthalapurana. In other words, to recreate English within that tradition of "legendary history." Whether Rao has been successful in doing so can be judged by critics who are competent to do so. Rao, however, does recognize that it is India's Puranas and epics that provide ideas for structural frameworks to him: the conventions of *Kadambari* (7th century CE) by Bana, and *Uttararamacharita* (7th century CE) by Bhavabhuti. One is, therefore, not surprised that Rao regrets his inability to write in Sanskrit. And he often talks about it with nostalgia.

In 1997, in *The Vintage Book of Indian Writing 1947-1997*, Salman Rushdie, commenting on "the generation of independence, Midnight's parents" of Indian English, rightly calls them "the true architects" of a new tradition (eg, Mulk Raj Anand, R K Narayan, Raja Rao). Rushdie considers Rao "... a scholarly Sanskritist, [who] wrote determinedly of the need to make an Indian English for himself, but even his much-praised portrait of village life, *Kanthapura*, seems dated, its approach at once grandiloquent and archaic" (1997a: xvii). These are, of course, broad and sweeping generalizations. But then, a few pages earlier (xi), Rushdie is honest when he says that some readers [of the anthology] may feel that "we are simply betraying our own cultural and linguistic prejudices, or defending our turf, or – even worse – gracelessly blowing our own trumpet" (xi).

In the same volume, Rushdie, however, does echo Rao's observation of 1938 that "Indian English, sometimes unattractively called Hinglish, is not English English, to be sure, any more than Irish or American or Caribbean English is." The achievement of the writers is "... to have found literary voices as distinctly Indian, and also as suitable for any and all of the purposes of art, as those other Englishes forged in Ireland, Africa, the West Indies, and the United States" (1997a: xiii).

In Rao's "Author's Foreword" *to Kanthapura* he says that "our paths are interminable." And he elaborates, "We have neither punctuation nor the treacherous 'ats' and 'ons' to bother us – we tell one interminable tale."

Rao, as indicated above, has no hesitation in violating the traditional conventions of English punctuation, capitalization, and sentence construction. In the traditional orthographies of Indian languages there are just viram and ardhaviram, one represented by one vertical line and the other by two such lines. There are, therefore, no rules of Fowler's prescriptivism for Rao, though Fowler had acquired the status of a linguistic Bible in colonial Asia and Africa.

In *The Chessmaster and His Moves*, for example, Rao is indifferent to the conventions of English punctuation, capitalization, and sentence and discourse organization. There are sentences of one page (264-65) and even one and a half pages in length (501-2). There is a conscious attempt to extend the Indianness of the language by de-emphasizing its "alien" canonical conventions – the Judeo-Christian conventions, the range of linguistic and contextual associations that identifies English with Western canons. What Rao does is to put India's English on the same linguistic pedestal as Sanskrit, which has been in Rao's native India for the past thousands of years. And Rao does it on his own terms. That is what he had envisioned in 1938 when he said:

> Our method of expression therefore has to be a dialect which will someday prove to be as distinctive and colourful as the Irish or the American. Time alone will justify it.

What Rao said in 1938 in those four hundred and sixty one words was both visionary and prophetic. It was the first conceptualization of the canonicity of India's English. It was visionary in more than one sense. In his approach to Imperial English he was creative and assimilative. He questions the pragmatics of the exocentric model; argues for the legitimacy of the nativization of English, and justifies the acculturation of Imperial English to give it an Indian identity. In other words, he locates the language in India's linguistic and cultural space.

Rao's Credo in a Historical Context

In the historical context of world Englishes, the crosscultural spread and emerging new identities and canons of English, Rao's credo was indeed, to repeat Parthasarathy, "revolutionary." In the 1930s, and until much later, Imperial English continued to have a firm grip — attitudinal and symbolic — on all world varieties of English. One has to make a distinction here between attitudes toward the Received variety of English and actual performance in the variety. In literature, it has been shown that even in the USA, UK and other Inner Circle countries, adherence to the Received model has been an exception and not a rule. And in recent years "the loose canons" are aggressively seeking their legitimate linguistic rights in that mythical circle. But that is a different story.

One might ask: What were the views on "linguistic liberation" and experimentation in Rao's India and beyond in the 1930s? What was the context of English in the Outer Circle (Anglophone Asia and Africa)? Rao made these observations just nineteen years after Henry

Louis Mencken (1880-1956) published his monumental *The American Language* (1919). In his first edition of the book, Mencken claimed that

> ... Americans spoke a separate language of their own making that they could take pride in, not an imperfect imitation of the language of England (McArthur 1992: 651; see also Kahane 1992).

The stirring for an identity had just begun in the USA, but Australia, New Zealand, and Canada were still not seeking an autonomous linguistic identity in any serious sense. The story of English in the Outer Circle was essentially one of English as the tool of the Empire. The Empire had yet to become articulate in English. It is true that bilingualism in English had gradually gained momentum, but there was still no recognition of the types of crossover, or markers of new linguistic and cultural identities for the language.

A parallel example of the linguistic – and cultural – appropriation of English by the natives of the Outer Circle would be that of Africa. However, in the 1930s, the Africanization of English and its exponents of identity had yet to be established. We see the first articulation of that in a most skilful way in, for example, Amos Tutuola in the 1950s and Chinua Achebe in the 1960s. That is almost three decades after Rao's Foreword. The insightful argument of Achebe about "how I approach the use of English" reveals the most skilful argument of a literary craftsman. In making a case for the Africanization of English, Achebe contrasts the Africanized version with "another way" – the non-Africanized way. In Achebe's *Things Fall Apart* (1966), the chief priest, explaining to one of his sons the importance of sending him to church, says to him in what may be called the Africanized version:

> I want one of my sons to join these people and be my eyes there. If there is nothing in it you will come back. But if there is something then you will bring back my share. The world is like a mask dancing. If you want to see it well, you do not stand in one place. My spirit tells me that those who

do not befriend the white man today will be saying "had we known," tomorrow.

Then Achebe contrasts this with another version – a non-Africanized version – and asks, "supposing I had put it another way. Like this for instance":

> I am sending you as my representative among these people – just to be on the safe side in case the new religion develops. One has to move with the times or else one is left behind. I have a hunch that those who fail to come to terms with the white man may well regret their lack of foresight.

In support of the first version – the African version – Achebe provides a pragmatically and contextually valid argument. In his view, "... the material is the same. But the form of the one is in character, the other is not. It is largely a matter of instinct but judgment comes into it too."

The two crucial words here are "instinct" and "judgment": the first relates to the African "thought-pattern" as transcreated into English and the second to pragmatism with reference to the African context. In Achebe's decision, we see that African "thought-movement" has not been "maltreated in an alien language." Indeed, Rao would agree with Achebe.

What we see, then, is that each African and Asian English-using country adopts a strategy relevant to its own contexts of culture and patterns of interaction. The theoretical dimensions of Englishization have been almost identical, but the specific linguistic innovations have varied in each region – West Africa, East Africa, Southern Africa, South and East Asia. The search has been toward the same end – to seek a culture-specific cultural identity through the medium of English.

The most passionate articulation of this position is in Wole Soyinka, who emphasizes that English plays "unaccustomed roles" in Africa and has thus become a "new medium of communication." This medium functions in "a new organic series of mores, social goals, relationships, universal awareness – all of which go into the creation of new culture."

Soyinka expresses the Africanization of English very differently from Rao when he says that:

> Black people twisted the linguistic blade in the hands of the traditional cultural castrator and carved new concepts into the flesh of white supremacy.

In this metaphor there is both passion and anger – the medium is an active weapon. And what used to be "the enslaving medium," as Soyinka sees it, has been converted into "an insurgent weapon." In other words, the acculturation and Africanization of English has been complete. The process which Soyinka explains in a way answers Gabriel Okara's (1963: 15-16) question:

> Why shouldn't there be a Nigerian or West African English which we can use to express our own ideas, thinking and philosophy in our own way?

The identity issue is not restricted to Asia or Africa – far from that. We see it in the USA too. The result is what Gates, Jr (1992) calls "the culture wars" for the identity of "the loose canons."[8]

The "Loose Canons" and Other Canons

What are the responses to the canons of creativity in English, in what was the Empire? What is the reaction to what Rao's 1937 [1938] credo has unleashed? The reactions have been of two types. The first reaction is that the multilingual's creativity in Asia and Africa has given the English language a unique vitality, innovation, and cultural expansion. It has given it a pragmatic legitimacy. The result is what may be called the "multicanons" of English – actually, Englishes. It has indeed rejuvenated the medium and rescued it from exhaustion. The other reaction is almost the opposite of that, as demonstrated in, for example, the attitudes andconcerns of Bailey and Quirk. I have discussed it in detail elsewhere.[9]

The on-going debate about diluting the canon and keeping "loose canons" out on the periphery is only one side of the current debate on English. Rushdie (1991: 61) encountered this attitude when a specialist in English literature, "... a friendly and perceptive man" suggested to him that

> ... [as] a Commonwealth writer ... you probably find, don't you, that there's a kind of liberty, certain advantages, in occupying, as you do, a position on the periphery?

This *periphery* is one way that "defines" a Commonwealth writer in English. At a seminar in Cambridge, a lady from the British Council reassured Rushdie that, "it's all right, for the purposes of our seminar, English studies are taken to include Commonwealth literature." (1991: 61) And Rushdie continues that

> ... [a]t all other times, one was forced to conclude, these two would be kept strictly apart, like squabbling children, or sexually incompatible pandas, or perhaps, like unstable, fissile materials whose union might cause explosions.
> (1991: 61)

Rao's mantra of the Indian reincarnation of English is one perspective. The debate about English in India, initiated with Macaulay's Minutes of 1835, has continued unabated. There are more than two sides to it. Consider, for example, views expressed in reviews. These views present two distinct visions and two distinct responses to Rao's mantra. First, the ecstasy of an Indian journalist, N S Jagannathan (1996):

> And the most important means that both the rulers and the ruled used for transforming the Indian mind and imagination was, ironically, the English language. It was through it we had access to Western (read English) ideas and imagination. And Sanskrit literacy among even educated Indians being what it is, it was through English that the majority of them discovered their own intellectual history including that part of it inscribed in Indian languages

unknown to them. Even anti-British nationalism was nurtured by English, a fact often forgotten by Macaulay-baiters assailing the hegemonic hold that the West has even today on our thinking.

Second, the agony of an Indian educator, R C Gupta (1996):

The ethical question: How and by what logic should we continue to impose English language on our young learners? and How much damage are we doing to the Indian languages and to the self-esteem of their speakers by our continued insistence on the teaching of English as an integral, nay essential, part of our curriculum? – are not asked even by one contributor.

Rao's Mantra and Caliban's Canon

There is no paucity of theoretical, ideological and pragmatic perspectives and analyses on the consequences of the introduction of English in Colonial Asia and Africa. And each label, each epithet and each characterization represents an underlying attitude and a vision of a nation, nationhood and national linguistic identity. These identities are reflected in the use of attitude-marking terms for English such as *auntie tongue, Trojan horse*, the *Other tongue, step daughter*, and so on.

The most suggestive and loaded metaphor indeed is Caliban's tongue. It symbolizes how Caliban acquired a voice and used it as a linguistic weapon. It also symbolizes the imperial attitude toward Caliban and what he represents. The language was used for the spiritual, moral and educational elevation of Caliban – Asia and Africa were the White Man's burden.

But not for Rao. He does not use any such metaphors. There is no Caliban here, nor is Rao using English from the periphery. He brings English, and its functions, to the centre of his creativity, to the centre of *Indianness*. In his hands, the crossover of the language is on Rao's terms.

In the Foreword to *Kanthapura*, Rao makes a calm assertion of the instrumental use of the English language without the anger and agony of Nigeria's Wole Soyinka or the accusation of racism against the English language of Kenya's Ngugi wa Thiong'o. There is no conscious linguistic overlay of, for example, Mulk Raj Anand (1998), nor is there any "radical linguistic operation" of Salman Rushdie (cited in Langeland 1996:16):

> The (English) language ... needs to be decolonized, to be made in other images, if those of us who use it from positions outside Anglo-Saxon culture are to be more than artistic Uncle Toms. And it is this endeavour that gives the new literatures of Africa, the Caribbean and India much of their present vitality and excitement.

When asked, "Why does Rao use English?"[10] his response is consistent with the historical context of the period and within the assimilative linguistic tradition of India's past. He says:

> Historically, this is how I am placed. I'm not interested in being a European but in being me. *But the whole of the Indian tradition, as I see it, is in my work.* There is an honesty in choosing English, an honesty in terms of history [emphasis added].

Rao prefers the medium of English for pragmatic reasons too:

> In English, it seems as if one can do what one wants with the language. There are fewer rules, it's a newer language, and therefore has more freedom for invention.   (145)

And he contrasts English with French:

> I lived in France for a long time and know French almost as well as I do English, but this freedom is not available in French at all. French is so strict a language that there is hardly any freedom there.   (145)

We see the same view shared by Rao's younger contemporary, Anita Desai. Her "material" is "Indian" and she "had to bend it and adapt it somehow to the English language." Desai continues:

> The reason I'm so fascinated by the English language is that it's really possible to do this with English; it is flexible, it is so elastic. It does stretch, it does adapt, and it does take on all those Indian concepts and traditions and ways. (171)

The canon formation had begun with Rao and it continues in various ways in the postcolonial Indian writing in English.

Conclusion

The vision Rao presented in 1938 for India's English "as distinctive and colourful as the Irish or the American" has actually come true, especially during the post imperial period. It is meaningful that in 1988 Rao revisited the question which he had raised – almost as an aside – sixty years earlier. In *The Chessmaster and His Moves*, he brings in another facet, that of the contemporary English of his native India:

> Today of course what one speaks in India called English is a vernacular, and will someday grow like Urdu, taking its own rhythm and structure. (189)

And then Rao provides an Indian "meaning" to his contextualization, adding:

> We in India welcome everything outlandish and offer it to the gods, who taste it, masticate it, and give it back to us as prasadam ["offerings to the gods returned to man sanctified"]. When our English will have come to that maturity it might still achieve its own nationhood. Till then it will be like Anglo-Norman, neither French nor English, an historical incident in the growth of culture. After all, and we forget so easily, sister, India is hallowed with wisdom, antiquity, and history. (189)

Once English acquired the ritualistic sanctity of prasadam, the earlier dichotomy that Rao suggested in 1938 between the *emotional* and *intellectual* make up ceases. Indian English becomes an integral part of *being* – being an Indian.

We have seen several visions concerning canons of world Englishes—the South Asian, the East Asian, the West and East African, and the African-American. Rao's vision of 1938 is far from Caliban's vision, or Caliban's anger or his revenge. And in Rao's hands language is not a weapon. There is no remorse, there is no revenge.

> You taught me language, and my profit on't
> Is I know how to curse. The red plague rid you
> For learning me your language![11]

For Rao, English is linguistic prasadam and he enjoys it, he celebrates it. It is consistent with his native parampara. In a recent evocative book entitled *Empire of the Soul: Some Journeys in India*, Paul Roberts says (1996:271) that after

> ... Independence, however, Indian English said farewell to British English and began a life of its own. The British had shipped back a rich hand of linguistic booty over the years, too; many commonly used words ... were the offspring of what Khushwant Singh termed promiscuous couplings with Indian languages. Home alone, Indian English became even more flirtatious among so many exotic tongues, rapidly evolving into a form as distinct at times as, say, the Irish English of James Joyce, or the richly varied American English of Damon Runyon, or Thomas Pynchon, or Alice Walker.

Roberts has missed the mark; in a way Indian English said farewell to British English in 1938 when Rao wrote his credo for creativity.

And as the years have passed, we see that Rao's mantra established a subtle connection between the English language and India's linguistic and cultural parampara and its assimilative literary culture. It took English over half a century to become an exponent of India's literary culture. In this way, Rao authenticates what he said later – much later – in an interview:

> ... the important thing is not what language one writes in, for language is really an accidental thing. What matters is

the authenticity of experience, and this can generally be achieved in any language.[12]

What Rao's mantra did was to create what has been called "unselfconsciousness" about English, about creativity in this language, about Indianness. The new generation of Indian English writers such as Vikram Seth are celebrating it. He says:[13]

> Many Indians have become quite unselfconscious about the use of English. It doesn't have colonial associations for them. They use it as freely as their own language.

The various modifications and elaborations of Rao's mantra thus provide us with early insights regarding "canon expansion" in world Englishes. These insights have to be contextualized within the literary and linguistic theoretical conceptualizations of the time – from the 1930s to the 1990s. What is to happen beyond the millennium is not easy to guess – the crystal ball is still very misty.

In literary terms, the influence of the Romantics was dominant in the 1930s. The concept of transcultural and multilingual creativity, and resultant canons, was yet to be established in English. Forster (1970) succinctly explains the context:

> ... we have all been brought up to believe that each language has its mystery and its soul, and that these are very sacred things, in whose name indeed much blood has been shed in our own lifetime and is still being shed ... [I]f we put sentiment aside, there are very many people and very many situations for which different languages are simply tools appropriate to certain definite purposes, analogous to the different stylistic levels within any one language.

This attitude resulted in what Lefevre (1990: 24) has called the attitude of "monolingualization" of literary history. He says it is

> ... another pernicious outgrowth of the "monolingualism" of literary history by Romantic historiographers intent on creating "national" literatures preferably as uncontaminated

as possible by foreign influences.

In linguistic conceptualizations, as Haugen (1950: 272) reminds us, the attitude toward a bilingual's creativity conveyed psychological and linguistic marginalization. What we see, as Haugen says, is that "... both popularly and scientifically, bilingualism was in disrepute." Haugen makes a poignant observation that "just as the bilingual himself often was a marginal personality, so the study of his behaviour was a marginal scientific pursuit."

It is within the context of such a literary and linguistic theoretical vacuum that Rao's mantra has to be contextualized. In canon-formation in world Englishes, in constructs for such creativity, and in understanding the bi- or multilinguals' linguistic behaviour, Rao's mantra insightfully reminds us that language is merely the madhyama.

In a multilingual's creativity, as Rao rightly observes, what language one writes in "is an accidental thing." The important thing is the "authenticity of experience." Rao believes that one can express one's "experience" through the madhyama of English. He "found English to be the nearest equivalent to ancient Sanskrit as it has almost the same range of varied expression, suppleness, and adaptability to different modes and effects and similar richness and complexity."[14] Rao found French "... far more disciplined and precise. It allowed less room for experimentation which he had to do to adapt a Western language to his Eastern sensibility."[15]

It is in this way – a pragmatic way – that Rao authenticates the formal and functional Indianness in Indian English. It is such authentication that contributed toward developing "strategic constructs" for the Indian canon of English. And it is through such constructs, to use Kermode's concept,[16] that a parampara is established, and that is what Rao did by using the subtle device of the "sacred thread" that Indianized the English language. It laid the foundation for the later generation – for example, the Rushdie generation and "Rushdie's children."[17]

Notes

1. An earlier version of this paper was presented at a symposium on "Word as Mantra: The Art of Raja Rao," at the University of Texas at Austin, USA, on 24 March, 1997.
2. I have used the New Directions paperback edition of *Kanthapura* published in 1967. The book was first published by George Allen and Unwin, Ltd, London, in 1938. Rao's "Author's Foreword" is dated 1937.
3. For a detailed discussion see, eg, Kachru, 1991, and 1996b.
4. See, eg, Padoux (1990: 372). For further analysis of literature on this topic see also Alper, ed 1989; and Gonda 1963; and Padoux 1988.
5. For references on English as a medium of plural canons and other related issues see Kachru 1997.
6. See Kachru 1995.
7. For other perspectives see also Dissanayake (1985), Kachru (1985, 1986, and 1991) and Thumboo (1985 and 1992).
8. See Gates, Jr 1992.
9. See Kachru 1991 and 1996a.
10. See Jussawalla and Dasenbrock (1992: 144).
11. William Shakespeare, *The Tempest*. Caliban, I, ii.
12. See Jussawalla and Dasenbrock (1992: 147).
13. Interview published in *India Currents* 7.3 (June 1993): 20.
14. Cited in Srivastava (1980: 106).
15. Cited in Srivastava (1980: 105-106).
16. Cited in Altieri (1990: 22).
17. See Amitav Kumar's review of *The God of Small Things* (Arundhati Roy) and *The Calcutta Chromosome* (Amitav Ghosh) in *The Nation* 265.9 (New York, 29 September, 1998: 36-38) with the caption "Rushdie's children."

Works Cited

Alpher, H P, ed. *Understanding Mantras*. Albany: State U of New York P, 1989.

Altieri, Charles. *Canons and Consequences: Reflections on the Ethical Force of Imaginative Ideals*. Evanston: Northwestern UP, 1990.

Anand, Mulk Raj. *The King-Emperor's English: Or the Role of the English Language in Free India*. Bombay: Hind Kitab, 1948.

Dey, Esha. "A Baroque Stylization: A Note on Raja Rao's *The Serpent and the Rope*." *Language Forum* 6.3-4. Delhi (Oct-Dec, 1980 - Jan-Mar, 1981): 1-15.

Dissanayake, Wimal. "Towards a Decolonized English: South Asian Creativity in Fiction." *World Englishes* 4.2 (1985) : 233-242.

Fernandez-Armesto, Felipe. *Millennium: A History of the Last Thousand Years.* New York: Scribner, 1995.

Forster, Leonard. *The Poet's Tongues: Multilingualism in Literature* (The de Carle Lectures at the University of Otago 1968). Cambridge: Cambridge UP (in association with U of Otago P), 1970.

Gates, Jr, Henry Louis. *Loose Canons: Notes on the Culture Wars.* New York: Oxford UP, 1992.

Gemmill, Janet. "The Transcreation of Spoken Kannada in Raja Rao's *Kanthapura*." *Literature East and West* 18.2-4 (1974): 191-202.

Goffin, R C. *Some Notes on Indian English.* S P E Tract No 41. Oxford: Clarendon Press, 1934.

Gonda, J. "The Indian Mantra." *Oriens* 16 (1963).

Gupta, R C. Review in *The Book Review.* Delhi (April, 1996).

Haugen, Einar. "The Analysis of Linguistic Borrowing." *Language* 26 (1950): 210-231.

Jugannathan, N S. Review in *The Book Review.* Delhi (April, 1996).

Jussawalla, Feroza & Reed Way Dasenbrock. *Interviews with Writers of the Post-Colonial World.* Jackson & London: UP of Mississippi, 1992.

Kachru, Braj B. The Indianization of English: The English Language in India. New Delhi: Oxford UP, 1983.

—. "Standards, Codification and Sociolinguistic Realism: The English Language in the Outer Circle." *English in the World: Teaching and Learning the Language and Literatures.* Ed R Quirk and H G Widdowson. Cambridge: Cambridge UP, 1985. 11-30.

—. "The Power and Politics of English." *World Englishes* 5.2-3 (1986): 121-140.

—. "The Bilingual's Creativity: Discoursal and Stylistic Strategies in Contact Literature." *Discourse Across Cultures: Strategies in World Englishes.* Ed Larry E Smith. New York: Prentice Hall, 1987. 125-140.

—. "Toward Expanding the English Canon: Raja Rao's 1938 Credo for Creativity." *World Literature Today (*Autumn 1988): 582-586. (Special issue "Raja Rao: Our 1988 Neustadt Prize Laureate".)

—. "Liberation Linguistics and the Quirk Concern." *English Today* 7.1 (1991): 1-13.

—. "English in South Asia." *The Cambridge History of the English language* V. Ed Robert Burchfield. Cambridge: Cambridge UP, 1994: 497-553.

—. "Transcultural Creativity in World Englishes and Literary Canons." *Principle and*

Practice in Applied Lingusitics. Ed Guy Cook and B Seidlhofer. Oxford: Oxford UP, 1995. 271-287.

—. (1996a). "World Englishes: Agony and Ecstasy." *Journal of Aesthetic Education* 30.2 (Summer 1996): 135-155.

—. (1996b). "The Paradigms of Marginality." *World Englishes* 15.3 (1996): 241-255.

—. "World Englishes 2000: Resources for Research and Teaching." *World Englishes 2000.* Ed Larry E Smith and M L Forman. Honolulu: U of Hawai'i P, 1997. 209-251.

Kahane, Henry. "American English: From a Colonial Substandard to a Prestige Language." In Kachru, 1992. 211-219.

Kermode, Frank. "Institutional Control of Interpretation." *Canons and Consequences: Reflections on the Ethical Force of Imaginative Ideals.* Ed Charles Altieri. Evanston, Illinois: Northwestern UP, 1979.

Kindersley, A F. "Notes on the Indian Idioms of English: Style, Syntax and Vocabulary." *Transactions of the Philological Society* (1938): 25-34.

Langeland, Agnes Scott. "Rushdie's Language: Agnes Scott Langeland Considers How Salman Rushdie Destabilizes the Western Bias in English." *English Today* 12.1 (January 1996): 16-22.

Lefevre, Andrea. "Translation: Its Genealogy in the West." In *Translation, History and Culture.* London and New York: Printer Publishers, 1990.

McArthur, A. *The Oxford Companion to the English Language.* Oxford: Oxford UP, 1992.

Mencken, H L. *The American Language.* New York: Knopf, 1919. (British ed: London: Routledge and Kegan Paul, 1941.)

Naik, M A. *Raja Rao.* New York: Twayne Publishers, 1972.

Narasimhaiah, C D. "The English Language in India." *Hemisphere* 8 (April 1964): 26-30.

—. *Raja Rao.* New Delhi: Arnold-Heinemann, 1973.

—. ed. *Awakened Conscience: Studies in Commonwealth Literature.* New Delhi: Sterling Publishers, 1978.

Nehru, Jawaharlal. "The Language Problem in India." *Bulletin of the Central Institute of English and Foreign Languages* 3 (1963): 1-6.

Okara, Gabriel. "African Speech ... English Words." *Transition* 10.3 (1963):13-18.

Padoux, Andre." Mantras, What Are They?" In Alper, ed. 1988.

Padoux, Andre. *"Vac: The Concept of the Word in Selected Hindu Texts."* Albany: State U of New York P, 1990.

Paikeday, T M. *The Native Speaker is Dead!* Toronto: Paikeday Publishing Inc, 1985.

Parthasarathy, R. "Tradition and Creativity: Stylistic Innovations in Raja Rao." *Discourse Across Cultures: Strategies in World Englishes.* Ed Larry E Smith. London: Prentice-Hall, 1987.
Rao, Raja. *Kanthapura.* London: Allen and Unwin. With an introduction by C D Narasimhaiah. Madras: Oxford UP, 1974 (2nd Edition).
—. (1978a). "The Caste of English." In Narasimhaiah, ed. 1978.
—. (1978b). *The Policeman and the Rose.* Delhi: Oxford UP, 1978.
Roberts, Paul William. *Empire of the Soul: Some Journeys in India.* New York: Riverhead Books, 1996.
Rushdie, Salman. "Commonwealth Literature Does Not Exist." In *Imaginary Homelands: Essays and Criticism.* London: Viking, 1996.
—. Introduction. *The Vintage Book of Indian Writing 1947-1997.* Ed Salman Rushdie and Elizabeth West. London: Vintage, 1997. ix-xxiii.
Sharrad, Paul. *Raja Rao and Cultural Tradition.* New Delhi: Sterling Publishers, 1987.
Shills, Edward. "Citizen of the World: Nirad C Chaudhuri." *The American Scholar* (Autumn 1988): 549-573.
Soyinka, Wole. *Art, Dialogue and Outrage: Essays on Literature and Culture.* New York: Pantheon Books, 1993.
Srivastava, Narsing. *The Mind and Art of Raja Rao.* Bareilly: Prakash Book Depot.
Thumboo, Edwin. "Twin Perspectives and Multi-ecosystems: Traditions for a Commonwealth Writer." *World Englishes* 4.2 (1985): 213-22.
—. "The Literary Dimension of the Spread of English." *The Other Tongue: English Across Cultures.* Ed Braj B Kachru. Urbana: U of Illinois P, 1992: 255-282.
Whitworth, George C. *An Anglo-Indian Dictionary: A Glossary of Indian terms used in English, and of such English or other non-Indian terms as have obtained special meanings in India.* London: Kegan Paul, 1885.
—. Indian English: *An examination of the errors of idioms made by Indians in writing English.* Letchworth, Herts: Garden City Press, 1907.

YAMUNA KACHRU

CONTEXT, CREATIVITY, STYLE:
STRATEGIES IN RAJA RAO'S NOVELS

This paper explores the relationship of the Indian sociocultural context and creativity in style in Raja Rao's novels. This seems a worthwhile pursuit in view of the fact that most critics have made explicit observations about, for instance, the vernacular style of *Kanthapura* and the Sankritized style of *The Serpent and the Rope* and *The Chessmaster and His Moves* (eg, Dissanayake 1988, B Kachru 1988, Nagarajan 1964, Parthasarathy 1988). There has, however, been no detailed textual analysis of the exponents of vernacularization or Sanskritization of the English language in any of Rao's works.[1] I would also like to determine whether the concepts of vernacularization and Sanskritization are relevant only to the linguistic level in discussing Rao's style, or if they have implications beyond the linguistic items, that is, if the style features create the larger sociocultural context of India in English.

This paper is limited to a partial analysis of two novels: *Kanthapura* and *The Serpent and the Rope*. It has been suggested that whereas

Kanthapura has the characteristics of "living folklore" (Mukherjee 1971: 38) which "evokes the spirit and discourse of the oral tales of the eloquent vernacular" (Parthasarathy 1988: 561), *The Serpent and the Rope* represents the "Brahminical India" (Mukherjee 1971: 91) and has a "learned" style that results in "the Sanskritization of English" (B Kachru 1988: 584). In other words, both novels are inextricably linked to the Indian sociocultural context and their styles manifest both linguistic and cultural crossover. *Kanthapura* follows the conventions of the "little tradition" whereas *The Serpent and the Rope* those of the "great tradition."[2] This paper, then, is an attempt at ascertaining the exponents of Indian "cultural themes" (in the sense of Spradley, 1980) in the so-called simple, "unsophisticated" narration and verbal exchanges in the former, and the more complex, "sophisticated" narration, conversations, and debates in the latter work.[3] A related aim is to demonstrate that vernacularization and Sanskritization are processes that are complex and not confined to linguistic elements per se.[4]

In an interview in 1992, Rao says "[T]here are about two levels to *Kanthapura* and about eight to *The Serpent*" (Jussawalla and Dasenbrock 1992: 154). Uncovering and characterizing the levels must wait for a longer study, I will concentrate on two distinct cultural themes in the novels under focus, one universal in some sense, one more specific to Indian society and culture. The first theme relates to what may be termed "politeness" in social interaction, the second to "widowhood" in the Indian sociocultural context.

But before proceeding with data analysis and showing the impact of sociocultural context on some features of style, it may be useful to briefly define the terms "culture" and "style." Following Geertz (1983), culture can be viewed as "an historically transmitted pattern of meanings embodied in symbolic forms by means of which men [and women] communicate, perpetuate, and develop their knowledge about the attitudes towards life" (89). Style can be defined as a speaker/writer's choice of linguistic elements, a patterning of linguistic elements with relevance to the literary work in which such patterning occurs (Halliday 1974), and "making strange" (Erlich 1955) and "foregrounding" (Mukarovsky 1970) specific linguistic items, all of which create an effect.[5]

I will first situate my analysis of politeness in conversational exchanges within a theoretical framework. Then I will refer to select sociocultural factors, especially those related to the settings and participants.[6] Subsequently, I will discuss the themes of politeness and widowhood in Indian culture and society and its treatment in Rao's two novels.

The Concept of Politeness

Although polite behaviour is universal, the set of semantic features that make up the concept of politeness is not universal, and neither are the linguistic and other behavioural strategies adopted to signal polite behaviour. I am particularly concerned here with linguistic exponents of polite behaviour, though the larger setting and factors associated with participants, such as body posture, body movement, and gestures also play an enormously significant role. For instance, the folding of hands at the chest level accompanies the utterance of the item "namaste" for greeting in the Hindi-speaking community, bowing from the waist is an essential part of greeting in the Japanese culture, and the shaking of hands along with appropriate linguistic formulae is part of Western greeting patterns.

The linguistic expressions involved in polite behaviour comprise language-specific politeness formulae (Jespersen 1933: 266, Ferguson 1976: 138), which utilize particular instruments of politeness such as titles, kinship terms, honorific pronouns, plural markers, questions, hedges, etc. (D'souza 1988). Before discussing the stylistic use of these devices in Rao's novels, it may be useful to consider briefly the Indian notion of politeness.

There is no exact translation equivalent of the English word "politeness" in the Indian languages that I am familiar with. These include Bengali, Hindi, Marathi, Sanskrit, and Urdu. It has been suggested that politeness can best be expressed by terms such as a maryada, salinata, sila, sistata (and, possibly, bhadrata) borrowed from Sanskrit into Hindi.[7] These, however, are not exact equivalents of politeness, as is clear from the listings of English equivalents to these items in bilingual dictionaries. I reproduce below the equivalents to the terms listed above given in a standard Sanskrit-English bilingual dictionary:[8]

 1. maryada: boundary, limit, bounds or limits of morality and propriety, propriety of conduct
 salinata: modesty, humility
 sila: good disposition, integrity, morality, piety, virtue, moral conduct
 sistata: culture, learning, refinement (Monier-Williams 1899)

Whereas the meanings of refinement and consideration for others seem to be universal properties of what is meant by politeness, in the Indian context, two additional, equally essential characteristics are modesty and humility. Some evidence for this is found in verbal expressions that exalt the addressee at the expense of the addressor. It is the notion of modesty that dictates that one is not supposed to accept a compliment with an expression of gratitude; rather, one is supposed to deny that the compliment is deserved. Or, the acceptance has to be downgraded by some remark that shifts the focus to some other factor. An exchange such as the one cited below is common in most Indian languages:

 2. A. You have such a talented daughter. I understand she already completed her PhD by the age of 22.
 B. It is all God's grace.

Speaker B makes it very clear that it is not his/her daughter's intelligence or hard work, but God's grace which is responsible for the girl's success.

A typical example of humility is an utterance such as the following in a formal context in the Hindi speaking community:

> 3. Kabhi hamari kutiya me bhi padhare
> Please come (honorific) to our (humble) cottage some time.

The addressor may live in a mansion, but will refer to his/her abode as a "thatched cottage" in order to show humility and use a lexical verb from the "high" style to express the meaning of "come" to exalt the addressee.

The properties that characterize Indian notions of politeness are manifest in the narration and verbal interactions in Rao's novels. I will illustrate my observation with a few examples from Rao's *Kanthapura* and *The Serpent and the Rope*.

Setting in the Two Novels

The setting of *Kanthapura* is a village in Karnataka on the Western Ghats of India, in an area rich in grains like rice, spices like cardamom, and other cash crops like coffee, sandalwood, sugarcane, and teak. The village is well settled and has separate quarters for brahmins, pariahs, potters, weavers, and sudras. As a fairly prosperous and well-populated village should, it has a temple devoted to the village deity, goddess Kenchamma, on the hill, and a temple devoted to goddess Kanthapurishwari on the main street promontory. Women in the brahmin quarter used to gather on the veranda of the prosperous widow Rangamma's house to discuss Vedanta with her learned father. Once the Ishwara temple was built, however, everyone went there to listen to the Harikatha.[9]

The setting in *The Serpent and the Rope* is more complex. It spans several locations in Britain (Cambridge, London, Oxford), France (Aix-en-Province, Montpalais, Paris) and India (Allahabad, Bangalore, Benaras, Mumbai, Delhi, Hariharapura, Hyderabad, Kodaikanal, Madurai, Mussoorie). The domains are also varied; they include homes, centres of learning (eg, Allahabad, Benaras, Cambridge, Oxford, Montpellier) and places of pilgrimage (eg, Allahabad, Benaras [Varanasi]).

Participants

The narrator of the story of *Kanthapura* is an old woman from the "Veda Sastra Pravina Krishna Sastri's family," a widow with neither a daughter nor a granddaughter. She is a familiar grandmotherly figure, with no formal education, but well-versed in the myths, legends, the social and ritualistic practices of her community, also possessing a flair for storytelling. She recreates the speech events and the speech of the characters involved in them with aptness, as is clear from the examples cited and discussed below.

The narrator in *The Serpent and the Rope* is the main character of the novel, Ramaswamy, a well-educated South Indian Brahmin, who recites verses from Sanskrit, English and French with equal facility. Ramaswamy is acutely aware of his heritage and traditions. He is an Indian living in France and viewing India from there. He is a complex character embodying four distinct voices (Dissanayake 1988: 600): the voice of a North Indian proud of his Himalayan and Gangetic heritage, the voice of a South Indian acutely aware of the composite Aryan-Dravidian cultural legacy that is relatively less Islamized or Westernized, the voice of a connoisseur of European cultural and intellectual traditions, and lastly, the voice of the questing Self seeking to integrate the other three and cleanse them in order to realize the deeper metaphysical truth. He, too, recreates the speech events and speech of the characters involved in his spheres of activity very successfully.

Politeness in Interaction

The comparision of a few excerpts from each novel should clarify what is meant by the characters in the novels recreating speech consistent with Indian sociocultural norms in the vernacular and Sanskritized styles.

The following excerpt is from *Kanthapura*:

> 4. Achakka, you are of the Veda Sastra Pravina Krishna Sastri's family, and is it greater for you to ask something of me, or for me to answer Yea? (5)

The context is that the narrator is introducing the protagonist "Corner-house Moorthy" who is like "a noble cow, quiet, generous, serene, deferent and brahmanic, a very prince" (5). Her only regret is that she has no granddaughter whom she could offer in marriage to Moorthy. The quote represents Moorthy's reply, should the imaginary conversation about the marriage of the granddaughter to Moorthy have taken place. The term of address, "Achakka," and the saying "is it greater for you to ask something of me, or for me to answer Yea" conform to the Indian sociocultural conventions of politeness.

First, the term of address, "Achakka." In the Indian sociocultural context, as in many others, the speaker normally addresses the listener as mother, brother, sister, or with some other term in social interaction. Even complete strangers may be thus addressed, eg, in a shop, the shopkeeper may use kinship terms to address a potential customer while bargaining over the merchandise. In many of the world's languages, including the Indian languages, "Uncle," "Aunt," "Older brother," "Older sister," etc, are appropriate terms of address in ordinary circumstances for familiar persons as well as strangers older than oneself. Some of the terms of address in addition to kinship terms used in *Kanthapura* are "learned maharaja," "learned one," "sahib," and "maharaja" for the superior in status, and terms such as "licker of your feet," "your humble servant" for self-reference by men in interaction with their superiors. The former represent the face-enhancement of the addressee, the latter the humbling of the self in interaction with superiors, a hallmark of polite language used in Indian languages – both Indo-Aryan and Dravidian.

The use of sayings is also important in social interaction. Using sayings, such as "is it greater for you to ask something of me, or for me to answer Yea," appropriately is a marker of awareness of tradition, sensitivity to context, and respect for one's predecessors – gods and humans alike. After all, according to the Harikatha – man, Jayaramachar, even Brahma, had used the saying in addressing the sage Valmiki when requested by the latter to send one of the gods to free Brahma's daughter, India, from foreign rule.

> 5. "O sage," pronounced Brahma, "is it greater for you to ask or for me to say, Yea?" *Kanthapura* (11)

And it echoes in Ramaswamy's reply to his recently widowed Little Mother when she worries about what is to happen to the family. She fears that now that his father is dead, his two sisters, both teenagers, may not be as willing to submit to the authority of a stepmother who is only twenty six years old.

> 6. "I am your son. It is for you to say, and for me to obey."
> *The Serpent and the Rope* (43)

This is the expected role of a son irrespective of the fact that he is older in age than his stepmother. And as head of the family for the moment, it is his responsibility to make sure his sisters understand the situation and obey their Little Mother.

> 7. ... I told Saroja, "I have become the head of the family now. And since I must return to Europe soon, Little Mother will be my representative, with the power of the baton and the bank account."
> "We obey," said Saroja, looking at me shyly.
> *The Serpent and the Rope* (45)

Saroja, though rebellious in her thoughts, is conscious of the norms of behaviour and signals her intention to obey her older brother, the head of the family, on more than one occasion.

One such occasion is the occasion of her marriage. The entire episode, which is narrated in twenty one pages (253-274), starts with Saroja wishing she were a European woman so that, unlike an Indian woman, she could be free (255). The dialogue between the brother and sister continues as follows:

> 8. "What freedom?" I exclaimed. "The freedom of foolishness. In what way, Saroja, do you think Catherine or Madeleine is better off than you?"
> "They know how to love."
> "And you?"
> "And we know how to bear children. We are just like a motorcar or a bank account. Or, better still, we are like a comfortable salary paid by a benign and eternal British Government. Our joy is a treasury receipt."

Further on, she continues:

> 9. You had better wait till you see any in-laws. They already think I'm a cloth in their washbasket: they'll know when to beat me against the stone, to make me white as milk. We girls are thrown to other families as the most intimate, the most private of our clothes are thrown to the dhobi on Saturday morning. Like cotton, we women must have grown on trees ..."

But, once the preparations are complete, she reassures her brother, the head of the family

> 10. "Brother, I shall bring but a fair name to the household. Do not worry." (269)

There is no rancour, no fury, no accusation in Saroja's remarks (in 8 and 10 above); it is as if she were discussing a social evil rather than her own immediate fate. Any hint that her marriage was arranged as a result of a hasty or convenient decision on the part of Little Mother or Ramaswamy would have crossed the boundaries of propriety. And once the marriage is settled, the only concern a well brought up girl has is to "bring a fair name" to her natal family.

Unlike these conversations within the domain of the family in India, the conversations in *The Serpent and the Rope* often represent the samvada of the Upanishads. Metaphysical discussions are interspersed with the story line. The dialogue in 11 below from *The Serpent and the Rope* is an example of this "appropriating for fiction the domain of metaphysics" (Parthasarathy 1988: 562):

> 11. "As the Great Sage has said: In experience there is no object present. There is only experience."
> "Well, how is that?"
> "The sensation must finish its function before knowledge dawns. In Knowledge there is no object present – if so, who has knowledge of it? You might say I. And I has the knowledge of the I through –?"
> "Through Knowledge," said Madeleine.
> "So Knowledge has knowledge of the I through Knowledge, which means Knowledge is the I."
> "Yes, that is so."
> "That is why sugar is not sweet but sweetness is sweet, or Georges is not a man but Man is Georges." (110)

The context is a conversation between Georges, Madeleine, and Ramaswamy in the latter's home in France. Georges had been with Father Zenobias at a monastery and had been discussing the theory of evil. He had said earlier: "Evil is fascinating, for without it there would be no good, no world, no Christ." Ramaswamy had countered this with the observation, "The good cannot know itself, any more than light can know itself." The excerpt quoted above explicates the same Advaita philosophical position as the following remark of Rao's (Jussawalla and Dasenbrock 1992: 144):

> 12. For a good Christian, evil is concrete. For a good Vedantist, there is no evil. In the Indian tradition, there is no evil.

Another example of this style of interaction is a conversation between Savithri and Ramaswamy:

> 13. "... To say electricity is such and such an equation, simply means electricity is electricity. It is just like saying I see a thing, or God is equal to X. When seeing goes into the make of form and form goes into the make of seeing, as the Great Sage says, What, pray, do you see?"
> "You see nothing or, if you will, yourself," answered Savithri, and I wondered at her instant recognition of her own experience.
> "Therefore, what is Truth?" I asked. By now we were near Fort Sarrasine at the edge of the plateau of Les Baux, with the whole of La Camargue beneath us.
> "Is-ness is the Truth," she answered.
> "And is-ness is what?"
> "Who asks that question?"
> "Myself."
> "Who?"
> "I."
> "Of whom?"
> "No one."
> "Then I am is?"
> "Rather I am am."
> "Tautology!" she laughed. (128)

The conversation continues in this vein for some more turns and finally, Savithri says:

> 14. "So, when I see that tree, in that moonlight, that cypress, that pine tree, I see I – I see I – I see I."
> "Yes."
> "That is the Truth," she said, as we turned and walked back to the village. (129)

The context is that Savithri and her brother arrive in France, the brother has to go back to London immediately, but Savithri has come to spend some time in Aix with Ramaswamy and Madeleine. Savithri and Ramaswamy are walking under the moon and Ramaswamy observes (126), "For her truth was not tomorrow or yesterday – that is why she scarcely ever referred to India; truth is wherever one is – for there is no anywhere or anywhen, but all *is*, for one is not." The conversation in 11-12 takes place when Savithri asks (127), "Tell me, is it possible always to speak the truth?"

One can provide more examples, all of which represent the Upanishadic style of dialogue. As Parthasarathy (1988: 561) observes, Rao "has put the novel to uses to which it had not perhaps been put before by exploring the metaphysical basis of writing itself; of, in fact, the word." Sanskritization in *The Serpent and the Rope* manifests itself in this weaving together of ancient Indian speculation on metaphysics and language with the narration of the story of Ramaswamy, Madeleine, and Savithri.

The cultural theme of widowhood in the two novels displays the same strategies.

Widowhood in the Two Novels

This theme is all-pervasive in Indian languages. There is no greater misfortune for a caste Hindu woman than widowhood. A widow is inauspicious and unfortunate in herself, and brings misfortune to whoever sees her first thing in the morning, or while embarking on a journey, or while beginning an auspicious ceremony. She loses her right to wear her hair long, dress well, wear jewellery, the sacred kumkum mark on her forehead, and flowers in her hair. She normally loses her right to her husband's property, and only a very lucky widow is treated kindly in her natal family and/or her husband's family. The theme recurs in sayings, folk songs, folk tales, fiction, movies and poetry. And widowhood has been the focus of many social reform movements in Hindu society in modern times.

The theme of widowhood receives strikingly different treatment in the two novels. The vernacular language used in *Kanthapura* reflects the prevalent prejudice against widowhood and widows in both narration and conversation.

> 15. Then Rangamma's sister, Kamalamma, came along with her widowed daughter, Ratna, and Bhatta rose up to go, for he could never utter a kind word to that young widow, who not only went about the streets alone like a boy, but even wore her hair to the left like a concubine, and she still kept her bangles and her nose rings and earrings, and when she was asked why she behaved as though she hadn't lost her husband, she said that that was nobody's business, and that if these sniffing old country hens thought that seeing a man for a day, and this when she was ten years of age, could be called a marriage, they had better eat mud and drown themselves in the river. Kamalamma silenced her and called her a shameless and wicked-tongued creature and said that she ought never to have sent her to school, and that she would bring dishonour to the house. Ratna would beat her clothes on the riverstones, beat them and wet them and squeeze them, and packing them up, she would hurry back from the river alone – all alone across the fields and the lantana growth. The other women would speak of the coming Rampur temple festival or of the Dharmawar sari which young Suramma had bought for her son's haircutting ceremony, and when Kamalamma was gone they would spit behind her and make this face and that, and throwing a handful of dust in her direction, pray for the destruction of the house ... *Kanthapura* (30)

The passage makes it apparent that Ratna, the child widow, incensed the whole village by violating the conventional norms of behaviour: she dressed too well, wore jewellery, spoke out against her critics, and flaunted her independence by going about her business alone. The same attitude is reflected in utterances such as the following:

> 16. "Why should a widow, and a childless widow too, have a big house like that? And it is not her father built it," said she. "It's my husband's ancestors that built it. I've two sons and five daughters and that shaven widow hadn't even the luck of having a bandicoot to call her own. And you have

only to look at her gold belt and Dharmawar sari. Whore!"

(4)

Waterfall Venkamma is jealous of her sister-in-law Rangamma because she is just as prosperous as Venkamma. What makes it even worse is that Rangamma allows her parents, who have no business to be living with their daughter, to share her house with her. Rangamma's father is learned and the villagers enjoy his reading of "Sankara Vijaya day after day" (7), but that is of no consequence to Waterfall Venkamma.

The status of the widow lends itself to swear words such as the following in the village when there is "a battle of oaths" (59) between the police, and the villagers waiting for Moorthy:

> 17. "son of a widow" (59)

And when the news about Venkamma's daughter's forthcoming wedding is known and the village women, including the elderly widows and the child widow Ratna, start discussing what kind of a feast they will have, who will do what, and wear what:

> 18. ... Venkamma feels such esteem around her that she says to herself, "Ah, you widows, you will not even lick the remnant leaves in the dustbin, you polluted widows ..."
> (79-80)

Similarly, when the police arrive in the dark of the night to arrest Moorthy for following Mahatma Gandhi in using a spinning wheel to manufacture cotton yarn for his garments, and reading, and there is commotion in Rangamma's house, Venkamma's reaction is predictable:

> 19. ... and then comes the roar of Waterfall Venkamma, "Ah, you will eat blood and mud I said, you widow, and here you are!" (82)

When Rangamma goes to Advocate Sankara and stays with him to see how they could help Moorthy, who has been incarcerated, Venkamma is incensed:

> 20. And when Waterfall Venkamma heard of this she said, "Oh! this widow has now begun to live openly with her men," and she spat on the house and said this man had her and that man had her, and she began to say she would go to the courts and have back Rangamma's property, for land and lust and wifely loyalty go badly together, like oil and soap and hot water. (95)

In contrast, consistent with the refinement associated with Sanskritization, the theme is handled with great sensitivity in *The Serpent and the Rope*. The lexical item *widow* is not used anywhere. There are no direct references to widowhood in any of the conversations by anyone. Little Mother brings up the topic indirectly once by mentioning her husband's absence from their lives

> 21. " ... As long as He was there, there was someone to look after the house, and now I ask and wonder what will happen to everything ..." (43)

The use of "He" for the husband is noteworthy; no traditional Indian woman would refer to her husband any other way in conversation. Referring to one's husband by name is taboo; and expressions such as "my husband" violate the norms of social decorum.

The narration contains references to Little Mother's altered situation in passages such as the following

> 22. For Saroja I bought a simple white knitted sari from Lucknow. I wanted to buy bangles, too, but I was afraid they would break, and thought besides that when Little Mother had had to break them but the other day, to carry them would have been improper. (23)

One of the disturbing rites performed following the death of the husband is the breaking of the glass bangles on the wrist of the newly widowed woman. The above excerpt refers to the Little Mother's undergoing this upsetting experience following the death of Ramaswamy's father.

The following excerpt from the narrative has the same consideration and thoughtfulness:

> 23. When I came back after Father's illness I was too busy with doctors and visitors to think of being back home. I took Little Mother to the North, not to see India myself, but to show India to her and make her "inauspiciousness" familiar to herself. (46)

The simple phrase "make her inauspiciousness familiar to herself" speaks volumes. A new widow finds herself suddenly in a position where she is considered "inauspicious" and shunned on all festive occasions. It is a shattering experience in familiar surroundings, with the sudden change in attitudes and behaviour of kin and friends. As a considerate son, Ramaswamy thinks of visiting places of pilgrimage in the North, fully conscious of the fact that such places have a large number of widows living out their lives devoting themselves to meditation, worship, and other religious activities. Also, he hopes that the distance from familiar surroundings will afford Little Mother a chance to adjust to her changed circumstances, and that the relief of returning home after an absence will probably take away some of the anxiety resulting from her recent widowhood and the subsequent change in her relatives' and friends' behaviour.

The indirect references to widowhood in the narrative are thus in terms of a rite – the breaking of bangles, and a social conceptual category– the inauspiciousness of widows.

Conclusion

The brief discussion of a few examples from the two novels shows that vernacularization and Sanskritization are not mere linguistic processes. These processes represent two ways of experiencing the world. Vernacularization is appropriate in expressing the social world of folklore whereas Sanskritization is involved in characterizing a great tradition and the search for Truth. Vernacularization and Sanskritization, then, result in the two styles associated with *Kanthapura* and *The Serpent and the Rope*; the styles that "incarnate," in Thumboo's words, "the thoughts and emotions of characters ranging from relatively 'simple' peasants to the Brahmin prone to disquisitions" (1998 : 532). The styles manifest themselves in the characteristic use of language at the grammatical, ("Is-ness is the Truth, I see I"), lexical ("anywhen; son of a widow; remnant leaves") and idiomatic levels ("it is for X to say, for Y to obey; X is like cloth in Y's washbasket"). What is of greater consequence to the Indianization of English, is that they manifest themselves in the many cultural themes (eg, family, women, marriage, pilgrimage, Vedantic philosophy, etc).within the two themes I have briefly illustrated in this study. It is through such an acculturation that the process of "Indianization" was initiated which, eventually, in the 1990s, resulted in an Indian canon of the English language and literature.

Notes

I am honoured to dedicate this study to my respected friend, Raja Rao.

1. The well-known sociologist, M N Srinivas, defines Sanskritization as "the process by which a 'low' caste or tribe or other group takes over the customs, ritual, beliefs, ideology and *style of life* of a high, and in particular, a 'twiceborn' (*dwija*) caste" (1989: 56; emphasis added). This definition makes it clear that Sanskritization is a complex concept, including Sanskritization of language, but not confined to it. Sanskritization, like modernization as a conceptual category, affects the style of life in all domains, as research in anthropology, linguistics, and sociology, to mention just a few disciplines, has shown.

2. Anthropologist McKim Marriott (1955) defines the concepts of "great" and "little" traditions in the context of religious practices in village India by linking them to the concept of Sanskritization of Srinivas (1952). Religious practices that depend upon Sanskrit works which have a universal spread all over India for their authentication belong to the great tradition. More local practices with no such authority in Sanskrit works belong to the little tradition. See Ramanujan (1973: Introduction) for a discussion of the "great" and "little" traditions in Indian literature.

3. According to Spradley (1980), a cultural theme is a principle recurrent in a number of domains, tacit or explicit, and serving as a relationship among subsystems of cultural meaning. Themes are assertions that have a high degree of generality within the culture.
4. It is impossible to deal with even one of the two works comprehensively in the limited space of a paper. As such, this discussion represents just an initial attempt at exploring the topic.
5. The concepts of "making strange" (*priem ostranenija* of Russian formalists), and "foregrounding" (Prague Linguistic Circle) are discussed in Erlich (1955) and Mukarovsky (1970), respectively.
6. The discussion of data in this study is based on the theoretical frameworks of interactional sociolinguistics (Gumperz 1982, Tannen 1984) and the ethnography of speaking (Hymes 1974).
7. Y Kachru (1992), Pandharipande (1992) discuss the Indian notion of politeness in some detail. The terms used in Y Kachru (1992) are maryada (Sanskrit) and lihaj (Perso-Arabic); the term used in Pandharipande (1992) is maryada. According to Monier-Williams (1899), bhadrata means "honesty, probity," and bhadra vac is "pleasant speech."
8. All of these items are polysemous; I have listed only the equivalents relevant to the discussion of politeness.
9. Harikatha refers to a performance in which a learned storyteller narrates episodes from the story of a major deity (eg, Krishna) drawing upon sources such as the Bhagawat Purana and devotional literatures of Indian languages. Puranas, "ancient stories," are a class of sacred works, eighteen in number, that contain historical events, legends, myths, and stories of creation and evolution of the universe.

Works Cited

Dissanayake, Wimal. "Questing Self: The Four Voices in *The Serpent and the Rope.*" *World Literature Today*, 62:4 (Autumn 1988): 598-602.

D'Souza, Jean. "Interactional Strategies in South Asian Languages: Their Implications for Teaching English Internationally." *World Englishes* 7 (1988): 159-171.

Erlich, Victor. *Russian Formalism: History-Doctrine.* The Hague: Mouton, 1955.

Ferguson, Charles. "The Structure and Use of Politeness Formulas." *Language in Society* 5, (1976): 137-151.

Geertz, Clifford. *Local Knowledge.* New York: Basic Books, 1983.

Gumperz, John J, Jr. *Discourse Strategies.* Cambridge: Cambridge UP, 1982.

Halliday, M A K. "Linguistic Function and Literary style: An Inquiry into the Language of William Golding's *The Inheritors.*" *Literary Style: A Symposium.* Ed Seymour Chatman. New York & London: Oxford UP, 1974: 330-365.

Hymes, Dell. *Foundations in Sociolinguistics: An Ethnographic Approach.* Philadelphia: U of Pennsylvania P, 1974.

Jesperson, Otto. *Essentials of English Grammar.* London: Allen and Unwin, 1933.

Jussawalla, Feroza and Reed W Dasenbrock. *Interviews with Writers of the Postcolonial World.* Jackson and London: U of Mississippi P, 1992.

Kachru, Braj B. "Toward Expanding the English Canon: Raja Rao's 1938 Credo for Creativity." *World Literature Today* 62.4 (Autumn 1988): 586-587.

Kachru, Yamuna. "Speech Acts in the Other Tongue: An Integrated Approach to Crosscultural Research." *World Englishes* 11.32-3 (1992): 235-240.

Marriott, McKim. *Village India: Studies in the Little Community.* Chicago: The U of Chicago P, 1955.

Monier-Williams, Monier. *A Sanskrit-English Dictionary.* Oxford: Oxford UP, 1899. [Rpt Delhi: Motilal Banarsidas, 1990.]

Mukherjee, Meenakshi. *The Twice Born Fiction: Themes and Techniques of the Indian Novel.* New Delhi & London: Heinemann, 1971.

Mukarovsky, Jan. "Standard Language and Poetic Language." *Linguistic and Literary Style.* Ed Donald C Freedman. New York: Holt, Rinehart and Winston, Inc, 1970: 40-56.

Nagarajan, S. "An Indian Novel." [A review of *The Serpent and the Rope.*] *Sewanee Review* 72.3 (Summer 1964): 512-17.

Pandharipande, Rajeshwari. "Defining Politeness in Indian English." *World Englishes* 11.2-3 (1992): 241-250.

Parthasarathy, R. "*The Chessmaster and His Moves*: The Novel as Metaphysics." *World Literature Today* 62.4 (Autumn 1988): 561-566.

Ramanujan, A K. *Speaking of Siva.* Harmondsworth: Penguin Books, 1973.

Rao, Raja. *Kanthapura.* London: George Allen and Unwin Ltd, 1938. [New York: New Directions Paperback, 1963.]

—. *The Serpent and the Rope.* London: John Murray, 1960. [New York: Pantheon Books, 1963.]

Spradley, J P. *Participant Observations.* New York: Holt, Rinehart and Winston, 1980.

Srinivas, M N. *Religion and Society among the Coorgs of South India.* Oxford: Clarendon P, 1952.

Srinivas, M N. *The Cohesive Role of Sanskritization and Other Essays.* Delhi: Oxford UP, 1989.

Tannen, Deborah. *Conversational Style: Analyzing Talk among Friends.* Norwood, NJ: Ablex, 1984.

Thumboo, Edwin. "Encomium for Raja Rao." *World Literature Today*, 62.4 (Autumn 1988): 530-533.

MAKARAND PARANJAPE

THE DIFFICULT PILGRIMAGE:
THE CHESSMASTER AND HIS MOVES AND ITS READERS

This essay attempts to show that *The Chessmaster and His Moves* has met with at least three types of responses from its readers. First of all, as my reading of its early reviews shows, the book was greeted with consternation, disappointment, even rejection, not just by critics hostile to Raja Rao, but also by his admirers. Some of these reactions stem from what we might call the problematique of Raja Rao, the unique features and peculiarities of his discourse, which makes not just *The Chessmaster* but many of Raja Rao's other texts arduous and challenging. I try to highlight and clarify some of these interpretative doubts and misgivings by reading Raja Rao against the grain, as it were, via two important critics, David McCutchion and Paul Sharrad. Finally, through my own understanding of the text, I try to reaffirm what I see as not just the text's, but Raja Rao's, exceptional achievements as a writer.

Raja Rao's widely awaited magnum opus, *The Chessmaster and His Moves*, was finally released in June 1988. The story of its publication is by no means commonplace. Since I have recounted it elsewhere, I shall not repeat it here. Suffice it to say that, by any standards, the publication of this book was a major literary event. *The Chessmaster*, moreover, is just the first part of an ambitious trilogy, the second and third parts of which are yet to be published.[1] It is only after the publication of the whole novel, which will extend to roughly 2000 printed pages, that a fuller interpretation can be attempted. At present, then, what I propose to do is merely outline certain approaches and entry points to this complex and challenging book. More specifically, in this paper, I propose to do three things: first, to uncover certain interpretative cruxes in *The Chessmaster* through a discussion of the reception of the book in India. Second, to touch on what might be termed Raja Rao's larger ideological project and, thus, to lead up to a preliminary interpretation of the text. And, finally, to offer what I consider to be three useful approaches which can further help to untangle the text.

Raja Rao, everybody would acknowledge, is one of the three leading senior Indian English novelists; the other two are Mulk Raj Anand and R K Narayan. Furthermore, going by the number of critical studies *The Serpent and the Rope* (1960) has attracted, one may argue that it is possibly the most influential and accomplished of Indian English novels. I can think of no other contenders to this title except G V Desani's *All About H Hatterr* (1948) or Salman Rushdie's *Midnight's Children* (1981). Yet, the former has not attracted the kind of attention that *The Serpent and the Rope* did, while the latter's reputation has yet to stabilize. After *The Serpent and the Rope* Raja Rao published, over several years, only two books, the highly acclaimed *The Cat and Shakespeare* (1965) and the disappointing *Comrade Kirillov* (1976). *Kirillov* had appeared in a French version much earlier, in 1965. Hence, *The Chessmaster* appeared twenty eight years after Raja Rao's last major book, *The Serpent and the Rope*, and twenty five years after the other two books. The award of the prestigious Neustadt Prize to Raja Rao when *The Chessmaster* was still awaiting publication only added to the anticipation and excitement built up over the long years of silence. To say the least, everybody expected something big – at last, the great Indian English novel! That is why I have found it useful and important to provide an account of the early reception of the novel. It is one way of conveying the interpretative problems and challenges that this accomplished, but difficult, text poses.

At the outset, however, I must clarify that in the following story of the reception of *The Chessmaster*, I shall be concerned primarily with its early reception in India. Hence, I leave out of my discussion the essays by R Parthasarathy, *"The Chessmaster and His Moves:* The Novel as Metaphysics" (561-566), and Edwin Thumboo, "Raja Rao: *The Chessmaster and His Moves* (567-573) in *World Literature Today* (Autumn 1988). This number was specially prepared to felicitate Raja Rao as the winner of the Neustadt Prize for 1988. It was published toward the end of 1988 and reached India only around March or April 1989. By then, all the reviews that I shall discuss had already appeared in India. Moreover, the articles that the special number contains were specially commissioned for this purpose and therefore belong, in proper, to a period prior to the general release of the book. Both Parthasarathy's and Thumboo's essays are useful as general introductions to the book and both stress its philosophical backgrounds. Parthasarathy's essay contains a survey of Raja Rao's earlier work, notes on the philosophical sources of the book as well as on some of its leading characters. It is neither an interpretation, nor a coherent reading of the novel. Thumboo's essay is more detailed and discusses the central philosophical issue of the novel, which he identifies as the quest for the Absolute. This essay also contains valuable insights into Raja Rao's characterization and narrative technique. Despite the fact that all the essays in this volume were commissioned, the occasional note of irritation cannot help creeping into some of them. Uma Parmeswaran, for instance, complains:

> Raja Rao the thinker seems a male chauvinist who identifies masculine sensibility with the male gender and feminine sensibility with the female gender and has carried this to

such an extent in his latest novel that it seems to be an insufferable heap of chauvinistic pomposity in which, moreover, all the literary flaws of his earlier novels – split plots, slow action, weak narrative devices such as diary entries, and imbalanced characterization – appear in a magnified form... Rao seems to have stretched out his recent novel into an endless ream of words so as to prevent even the most patient of readers from finding out that the core is just a hollow echo of his masterpieces of earlier years (574-577).

Parmeswaran's comments are in consonance with those of several Indian readers of the novel. To the best of my knowledge, apart from this special number, the book has not been widely reviewed anywhere in the Western press. Therefore, I might proceed straight to the book's reception in India.

Soon after its release in June, publicity copies were sent out to the major periodicals. By August, authorized excerpts and reviews started appearing in the Indian press. *The Illustrated Weekly of India* and *The Sunday Standard* carried excerpts, but no reviews. As far as I can ascertain, the first review to appear was by Girija Kumar in the Sunday *National Herald*, 7 August, 1988. The headline caption hailed the book as "A Major Work," and overall the review was positive. Yet Kumar acknowledged that the book was "difficult to read": its narrative "is not like a river in full flow, but like a sluggish stream meandering through shallow waters of numerous lagoons on the way to its ultimate destination." Kumar's review, however, made one extremely valuable point about Raja Rao's philosophical method in the book: "Everything is ultimately reduced to mathematical equations and indeed all gods are said to be mathematical formulate"[sic]. This statement shows a glimmer of the recognition of what I consider to be one of the most important techniques of the book. I shall come back to this point later.

Prolixity, tediousness, and repetitiveness – such charges have been made by many subsequent readers of the book, among them some of our leading Indian English critics. In a review which appeared in the Sunday edition of *The Tribune* on 28 August, K S Duggal said that Raja Rao's philosophical disquisitions, at times, "could be eliminated without injury to the action of the story." In a more influential review for *Indian Literature* (no 130, March-April 1989), M K Naik, after unfavourably comparing *The Chessmaster* with *The Serpent and the Rope*, accuses the novel of possessing "neither a solid thematic core nor a taut narrative" and of "general vagueness and confusion, drift and lack of precision" (177). A major critic of Indian English fiction said that she turned down the offer to review the book for the pre-eminent fortnightly, *India Today*, because she found it too long and unreadable. One of our senior-most critics and a long standing champion of Raja Rao, confessed to me that he found the book too long, and unnecessarily repetitious. Another leading academic of considerable authority quipped that reading the novel was like "walking in ointment."[2]

But it was the second review of the book by Prema Nandakumar for the venerable South Indian paper, *The Hindu*, published on 23 August, 1989, that really blew the lid off such more or less guarded criticism. Nandakumar's piece, entitled, "Polite passion of the bourgeois drawing room," is characterized by biting sarcasm and measured scorn. The review begins with a series of questions:

> Are we creating an age of false taste by championing with excessive zeal the cause of Raja Rao? Is he a Vedantic philosopher or an insufferable poseur? Is he the standard-bearer of the genuine Indian English style or the wrecker of the pliant language's spiritual possibilities?

The review goes on to argue, in a tellingly Tamil comparison, how much the *The Chessmaster* is really a rewriting of *The Serpent and the Rope*: "Old tamarind rice in new polythene bags." This is certainly an important point which was later picked up by Naik as well. But what makes Nandakumar's attack so damaging is that she implies that Raja Rao is a hypocrite, a fraud. Moreover, Nandakumar debunks Raja Rao's celebrated style, with its long sentences and multilingual erudition. About the latter she says: "Transliterated chunks from various languages are strewn around like undigested pieces of food in a gourmet's innards, and Raja Rao goes on and on mesmerised by his own voices[.]" Also, Nandakumar is put off by what she considers the book's weepy sentimentality that hints at a larger decadence. She reacts to "Desecratory images like copulation beneath the portraits of Sarada Devi and Ramakrishna Paramahamsa ..." Overall, the review is a sweeping indictment of Raja Rao.

Among the reviews that appeared in the Indian press, only one more remains to be discussed. This is by G S Amur, another respected critic and scholar. Published in the Sunday edition of *The Deccan Herald* on 9 October, the review is entitled, "Cosmic game that life is." Amur's review is different because he takes the book seriously and focuses on a major preoccupation of the novel, the dialectic between zero and infinity:

> Raja Rao's novels derive their structure from a dialectic between two levels of presentation, one operating horizontally and dealing with events in time and space and the other operating vertically through a celebration of truths transcending these dimensions.

The review ends abruptly, owing perhaps to the editor's scissors, and we are left without Amur's evaluation of the novel. The last item to appear on the book was written under the byline of Shiv K Kumar, an important writer and critic; however, it is not really a review but a report on the Neustadt Prize. It was published in the Sunday Magazine of *The Hindustan Times* on 4 December, 1988. Just one more comment, again negative, probably directed at the book, appeared in Khushwant Singh's famous column, "With Malice towards One and All" (*The Deccan Chronicle, 24 July, 1989):*

> There is also a strong element of narcissism in Raja Rao's long novels in which he barely conceals his identity as the handsome guru delivering sermons to his nubile chelis [female disciples] who in turn gratefully offer him all they

> have – tan (body), man (mind) and dhan (worldly wealth).
> Such nauseating self-esteem is mercifully absent in his short stories.

Singh is probably making a dig at Sivarama Sastri's relations with the four women in his life, Jayalakshmi, Suzanne, Mireille and Uma – all of whom he charms with his intellect and who are devoted to him. Uma, of course, is the stepsister, with whom Siva has a strong sensual, though not sexual, bond.

And after that there was a deafening silence. The book appeared to have sunk without a ripple. Just five reviews and a couple of more reports and excerpts for such an important book? Surely such a response is symptomatic of a larger problem that readers have with the work of Raja Rao. One could argue that the *The Chessmaster* has polarized the Indian English critical community into those who can't stand Raja Rao and those who love him; yet, perhaps it would be more accurate to say that the novel has exposed the contradictions in the critical response to Raja Rao as never before. For example, few of the writer's admirers have come out openly in support of the book. That is why I think that *The Chessmaster*, by being such an extreme example of a Raja Rao text, has highlighted certain problems.

Some of these problems were identified within a year of the publication of *The Serpent and the Rope* in a review by David McCutchion called "The Novel as Shastra."[3] I would like to go back to this essay briefly because I consider it one of the best ever written on Raja Rao's work. McCutchion starts with a Kiplingesque assertion:

> The whole idea that the great Indian novel is somehow going to "reconcile" or "assimilate" East and West is strangely misconceived, because the two approaches to life (and it is the approach that determines whether the novel is "Indian" or "English" are mutually exclusive.

McCutchion stresses the incommensurality of the Indian and the Western paradigms of reality. The question is, of course, whether this is true empirically or whether such antithetical constructions are ideological. This question assumes importance because Raja Rao himself is preoccupied with it. Later, I shall discuss his answers, which are surprisingly identical to McCutchion's, though framed differently. But what McCutchion seems to be questioning is the whole philosophy of synthesis and reconciliation between two systems which are, to him, totally incompatible:

> Considering that the novel's chief concern is circumstantial reality ... and that the traditional Indian viewpoint regards all this as tedious illusion, it may be questioned whether a truly Indian novel is at all possible. Raja Rao's book makes no attempt at half way solutions taking the "best" of both worlds: its sensibility and values are uncompromisingly Indian, absorbing all experience from the point of view of one who seeks Brahman.

McCutchion's identification of Indian tradition with a particular permutation of a particular philosophical system is questionable, so is his definition of the novel as a work whose chief concern is "circumstantial reality." Also questionable is his assumption that somebody who seeks Brahman, as Raja Rao's protagonists ostensibly do, cannot be concerned with circumstantial reality. In fact, Raja Rao's books contain a wealth of circumstantial detail, all of which is paradoxically put into the service of a view which denies ultimate reality to it. But McCutchion's basic point is still inviting. He implies that Raja Rao is terribly subversive in using the novel, which seems designed to convey "realism," to deny the ultimate reality of the phenomenal world. McCutchion points to two main features of *The Serpent and the Rope* which defy the conventions of the novel: first, "There is very little story ... Of the more than four hundred pages, few are narrative, most are meditation – an unhurrying philosophical soliloquy on the nature of reality ...." This observation is equally true of *The Chessmaster* if not more so. Out of the 700 odd pages, only a few help to advance the story. Second, the novel defies conventions of space and time, so necessary in the "ordinary" construction of reality. Hence, "distinctions and identities are blurred: Rama is a Vedantin. Wherever he may be – in Madras, Aix-en-Provence, Pau, or Bangalore – his thoughts are outside space and time." Again this is characteristic of Sivarama Sastri, the protagonist of *The Chessmaster*, as it is of Rama. Hence, McCutchion argues: "Since all is subjective illusion, there is no fixed reality upon which to build a novel, only a flux of impressions and interpretations." This too might be said with equal justice about *The Chessmaster*. McCutchion also observes that "too much solemn theorizing on the infinite can be a bore," the sort of point that the Indian reviewers of *The Chessmaster* seem to have made.

McCutchion locates the problematic of the book in its self-definition: how do we judge this novel? On its own terms or by the standards used to judge other novels?

> On its own terms Rao's book is hardly open to criticism: it is too long and repetitive; it is self indulgent, and undiscriminating; there is no development, it moves to no conclusion, ends where it begins. The major fault of the book is its philosophical garrulousness.

But toward the end of his essay, McCutchion suggests a way of dealing with the novel on its own terms, by exposing what he sees as "The contradiction at the heart of Rao's novel":

> Rama tries to live in the world and think out of it. This gives rise to a kind of duplicity tearing the reader and hero between double standards – desire for happiness and justice in this world, coupled with lack of responsibility and decision because this world is not ultimately real.

Thus it is McCutchion who first suggests a way of reading Raja Rao "against the grain," a method later taken up with much greater methodological exactness by Paul Sharrad in *Raja Rao and Cultural Tradition*. To sum up, the crux of McCutchion's criticism seems to be his problem with Raja Rao's subversion of the form of the Western novel:

> The question might arise: is this a novel at all? ... All the central concerns of the Western novel are absent – social relations, psychological motivation, characterization, judgement, a passion for the concrete ... Today, we would not be so worried on this score. It has become customary to suggest that the form of the non-Western novel is quite different from that of the Western novel. Also that such novels often defy all the conventions and devices of the Western novel. They are thus the repositories of alternate world views, of different realities. The notion of time, space, causality, individuality, and reality itself are as culture bound as are conventions of narrative.[4]

But in the process of offering what might appear to be an easily dismissible criticism of *The Serpent and the Rope*, McCutchion raises several crucial philosophical and interpretative problems that are suggested by Raja Rao's work. I shall refer to these later.

At this juncture, I had invoked McCutchion in order to make the point that all of his observations are as, if not more, true of *The Chessmaster* as they are of *The Serpent and the Rope*. When I say that perhaps they are "more true," I am merely trying to underscore the feeling that Raja Rao seems to have gone too far this time. While the earlier novel was praised and hailed as a classic, *The Chessmaster* seems to have been viewed as an embarrassment. Even faithful Raja Rao fans do not seem to have wanted him to go so far. It would seem that even a subversion of the Western novel should have its limits. Raja Rao seems to have delivered an impossible sort of book, a novel that is really an antinovel, a novel to end novels, a book that not only challenges, but actually resists reading in the normal sense of the word. In short, a book that makes impossible demands on its readers, strains their patience, and almost forces them to reject it.

I want to end this section with a review of my own experience of reading this book, so as to contrast it with the previous views. I think such an impressionistic recap has its uses, especially when attitudes to the book are still fluid and its interpretation has not yet become institutionalized.

The first reading was difficult. Until page 210, when Raja Rao introduces the theme of zero vs infinity, the former representing India and the latter the West, I found nothing really to hold on to. Siva's cerebrations seemed interminable and somewhat pointless. Like many of the other reviewers, I felt that I was back in the world of *The Serpent and the Rope*; the novel seemed to continue Rama's story, or was at least a more elaborate retelling of it. It was, at the same time, exciting to be back in Raja Rao's Paris. After page 210, the going was a little easier, until the last section of the book containing the much anticipated dialogue between the Brahmin and the Rabbi. This last section, I thought, was terribly tedious again. I kept marvelling at how nothing really happened in the novel. Even at the end the book is incomplete. We don't know what happens to Siva and Jayalakshmi or Siva and Suzanne. We don't know if Uma is finally cured of her sterility. Perhaps, all this is left for the next two parts of the trilogy. Overall, I thought that *The Chessmaster* was a slower, sadder book – much more ponderous and opaque than *The Serpent and the Rope*. What was most curious was that though the central characters were all in their thirties, they seemed so old, really aged and ancient, as if they had the knowledge in their bones that they were playing out their karmic chess game the millionth time; hence the depth of the weariness, of their dukkha, of their quiet, terrible, and deathly longing for liberation, moksa, or in the terms of the novel, for sunya, the zero, dissolution.

On rereading the novel, I found myself adjusting better to its pace. It demanded a different, unhurried, but concentrated attention span. This was not a book meant to be read by professionals, but by those with a deeper involvement in its central concerns. I was struck by its similarities with that other great text of Indian English poetry – Sri Aurobindo's *Savitri*. Like *Savitri*, *The Chessmaster* is a very ambitious book, which aims at expressing a totality. Raja Rao wants to subsume and encapsulate an encyclopaedic understanding of the world, as he sees it, in this book.

Like *Savitri*, I thought, this is a book that a lot of people will resist and ignore, but which can't be dismissed. Its very presence – so huge and solid – means that it cannot be brushed aside and rejected. Certainly, not with the ease with which some of the reviewers have done so. The central issue is not so much its "literary merit," because carping about a lack of plot, looseness of structure, or repetition, only exposes the limits of our own critical standards. Indeed, the book demands to be judged by its own standards, which most of the reviewers have failed to do. And even if the verdict is that "it doesn't work," such a verdict cannot be passed as facilely as Nandakumar and Naik have done.

To say, "I can't stand Raja Rao and all his philosophical dithering" is one thing; we are all entitled to our opinions and tastes. But therefore to dismiss his project as hypocritical or unsound is illogical and unfair. The critic must engage with Raja Rao on the author's own terms, even if he wishes to disagree with these terms; to show these terms to be self-contradictory, fallacious, or ambiguous is to begin a constructive (even in the deconstructive sense) engagement with the text. One thing I felt sure about after my rereading: Raja Rao is certainly not a poseur or a humbug. His involvement in the world of *The Chessmaster* is absolutely genuine. Why else would he re-cover and remap the same territory that he traversed in *The Serpent and the Rope*? If nothing else, I was sure that Raja Rao deserved to be taken very seriously indeed, certainly not to be rejected outright as some of the reviewers had done. *The Chessmaster* may not become a very popular novel, but it is certainly a major work. I hazard a prediction: as the years go by, we will see more and more criticism on this book and perhaps one day it will be recognized as an acknowledged classic, one of the great Indian novels of this century.

Before I offer the record of my own engagement with the text, I want to clarify that I do not intend to present a systematic reading here. That would be too ambitious for a paper of this sort. Instead, I would like to offer some broad guidelines or approaches to Raja Rao and

The Chessmaster. I think that these interpretative strategies should help open up the text to other readers.

Raja Rao's project is to show the viability of a world view which has been more or less eclipsed even from contemporary India. We might term this view Advaita Vedanta. More specifically, it is a tradition of wisdom exemplified in the Vedas and Vedanta, which was later systematized and popularized by its most impressive exponent and commentator, the great Sankara, and into which Raja Rao was initiated by his Guru, Sri Atmananda. The latter's method was to show that under all circumstances, at all times, the only reality, the only truth was the Absolute. He demonstrated this by reducing the world to its real state, which was merely the Absolute. An example of this method of reasoning can be found in a book such as *Atmananda Tattwa Samhita*. In this book, which is a transcription of dialogues, Sri Atmananda calls his logic "subjective" and contrasts it with the logic of the ancient Greeks, which he calls "objective"(119). It is this "subjective" logic which Raja Rao himself appears to use in his own work. One cannot, however, trace oneself back to the Source, the Absolute ground of being, until one has met the Guru. *The Chessmaster*, from such a perspective, merely prepares the ground for this transformative encounter. Only the Guru can show the way to the ultimate reality. The disciple believes that he is Siva because the Guru says so: "Desikotya sivovam," as Sri Adwayananda, the son and successor of Sri Atmananda, says in "Life Sketch of Sri Atmananda": "I am the Absolute through the words of my Guru"(xiii). But Siva's meeting with the Guru is still a long way off. It will take place in the volumes to follow. At present, Raja Rao's purpose is to show that nothing else, no one else but the Guru, can remove the dukkha that seems to permeate throughout human life. To that extent, *The Chessmaster* is merely an exploration of that primordial suffering. What happens to Siva, or for that matter anyone else, when he or she meets the Guru is beyond words. It is the sort of alchemy which must be experienced, but cannot be spoken of too easily. Raja Rao never, except indirectly, portrays or describes that momentous encounter. His novels only take one to the point when one needs, like the protagonists of the novels, to seek the Guru. Nothing else, no one else can satisfy.

The only way that Raja Rao can make this longing for the Guru philosophically viable is via a sort of modified existentialism. Advaita penetrates to the core of the flux that is the daily life of his characters, Ramaswamy of *The Serpent and the Rope* and Sivarama Sastri of *The Chessmaster*. These characters attempt to negotiate life in an Advaitic fashion, thus trying to demonstrate its efficacy in the contemporary world. This is somewhat like negating life even while one is living it, denying the ultimate reality of oneself even as one lives and suffers. That they succeed only partially is a part of Raja Rao's plan. Because only the Guru can demonstrate that there is absolutely nothing – no event, experience, feeling, or idea that can separate you from your true reality, which is the Absolute. It can be proven that at no point has there ever been a separation, falling off, or illusion. When the existence of illusion is disproved, the Right Absolute begins to shine by itself. Whenever illusion raises it head, it only serves to remind us of its unreality, and thence, of the ultimate Reality behind the illusion. Or, to put it succinctly, each object only points to That. Thus, in *The Chessmaster*, it is not the realization of self that is sought as in the earlier works, but a dissolution of self. No wonder its other major philosophical sources are the absolute monism of Sri Ramana Maharshi and the sunyavada of the Buddhist philosopher, Nagarjuna.[5] So, while Moorthy illustrates right action through Karma Yoga, Rama, Jnana Yoga or the path of knowledge, and Govindan Nair, a type of Bhakti Yoga, of complete self-surrender to the Divine, Sivarama Sastri represents the power of negative dialectics, the attempt not to achieve something, but to vaporize one's self into nothing. Here the familiar dichotomies between male and female, vowels and consonants, India and the West, Brahmin and Kshatriya, sage and saint, logic and devotion, truth and the world, all hinge on the opposition between zero and infinity. The Judeo-Christian tradition is shown to represent the quest for perfect society here on earth, which in India is seen as denying the validity of the world itself. The way out, for Raja Rao, is not to improve things as the saint-soldier does, but to dissolve contradictions completely. For him, all numbers dissolve into zero as they emerge out of it. Infinite is merely cumulative, while zero is total negation that cuts the root of illusion. One can never become perfect in time, but attain perfection only by negating time.

The only meaningful dialogue, for Raja Rao, is between the Brahmin (zero, dissolution, negation) and the Rabbi (infinity, completion, affirmation). The former is vertical, denying time; the latter is horizontal, finding fulfilment though time. It is such a framework that provides the skeleton of the plot of the novel. The first part, "The Turk and the Tiger Hunt," shows the incompatibility of Siva and Suzanne like that of Rama and Madeleine in the earlier novel; the second part is dominated by Siva's affair with Mireille; and the third with the dialogue with Michel, the Jewish holocaust survivor. The steadfastness of the Siva-Jayalakshmi relationship and the impossibility of its consummation, and Siva's relationship with his stepsister, Uma, and her inability to bear a child – these two relationships provide the glue that keeps the novel together. Moreover, there are the usual digressions, stories within stories, letters, diary extracts, and long, speculative internal monologues that characterize Raja Rao's narrative technique. A certain degree of novelty is offered in two or three characters whose role in the plot is minimal, but who are very important – Abd'l Krim, the exiled Algerian leader, and Ratilal the French Jain diamond merchant. Raja Rao had said in an interview that the book is a tribute and acknowledgement of the great suffering of the Jews on behalf of humankind; this is elaborated at length in the story of Michel. But the suffering of Michel does not make the world any more real for Siva; his solution for the world's problems still lies in self-extinction – not suicide, but an undoing of the self. *TheChessmaster* is neither an admission of defeat nor an affirmation of success; here we don't see either the failure or success of Advaita. *The Chessmaster* is an ambiguous book in which neither zero nor infinity wins. It accommodates not just the Brahmin and the Rabbi, but the Jain and the revolutionary – though the violent ways of the latter are viewed unfavourably through Gandhian eyes. *The Chessmaster* moves beyond these positions to a kind of indeterminacy. Siva, Raja Rao's spokesman, is no longer always right. Nor does he pretend to be in full control of his metaphysical project. There is always the more powerful presence of the Chessmaster behind the movements of the characters in the book. Of course, any notion of a personalized Chessmaster or prime mover is just another version of the God that Siva would deny as the quintessence of the horizontal. But this is one of the contradictions of the book.

I have provided above a broad and highly selective summary of my reading of the book. This will serve both as an invitation to the text and also as my apology for not engaging with it more directly. Below, I will provide a few approaches for interpreting the text, which I consider useful. First of all, it is useful to see the book, as the reviewers have pointed out, as a rewriting of *The Serpent and the Rope*. It is in the earlier novel that we can see the most convenient entry point to the central dialectic of *The Chessmaster*. Rama tells Savithri:

> Zero makes all numbers, so zero begins everything. All numbers are possible when they are in and of zero. Similarly all philosophies are possible in and around Vedanta. But you can no more improve on Vedanta than improve on zero. The zero, you see, the sunya, is impersonal; whereas one, two, three and so on are all dualistic. (205)

The Chessmaster picks up this opposition, between zero and infinity, the impersonal and the personal, the monistic and the dualistic:

> Either you accept the world, and build a human empire, accepting death and, therefore, the pyramids (whether you called it a mausoleum for Mao or for Tutankhamen), or you transcend the world and as such death itself, and find the Truth of Sankara's Sivoham, Sivoham. (145)

Or as Siva puts it cryptically in his dialogue with Michel: "The quarrel of man is between zero and infinity, between Truth – and God" (670). But what is important to realize is that the philosophical positions in *The Chessmaster* are more clearly defined and more neatly expressed. Not only are the thematic preoccupations similar, they are carried out by similar characters in both novels. Hence we can propose the following schema:

The Serpent and the Rope →	*The Chessmaster*
Ramaswamy	Sivarama Sastri
Madeleine	Suzanne
Savithri	Jayalakshmi
Savithri's husband	Jaya's husband,
Pratap	Surrendar
Anand (Savithri's brother)	Raja Ashok
Saroja	Uma
Subramanya Sastri	Ramachandra Iyer
Catherine	Mireille
Lakshmi	Rati
Grandfather	Father
Tante Zoubie	Madame X
Georgias	Michel
Lezo	Jean Pierre

The arrow mark indicates that the latter character has evolved from the former; sometimes the resemblances are so pronounced as to make them almost identical, while at the other end of the spectrum, as with Anand turning into Ashok, the former is merely a hint. In all cases, there is a strong relationship, either in the traits of the two that make up the set or in their functions in the narrative. Not just the central characters, but incidents, events, discussions, and locations, and even the quotations are common to both books. The resemblances are more than a sense of *deja vu* and it would require a detailed paper to discuss their implications. I only want to say that those who have read and enjoyed *The Serpent and the Rope* will find easier access to *The Chessmaster*; they will also have an added dimension of recognition as they read the latter text.

The second introductory tool has to do with Raja Rao's method of reasoning in *The Chessmaster*. Except for a hint in Girija Kumar's review, other readers have not been able to figure out whether or not there is a system to Sivarama Sastri's philosophical disquisitions. Is his erudition simply impressionistic badinage or does he work from some logical principles? Often, readers seem to be baffled by the numerous discussions in the book which seem vaporous, incoherent, and directionless. I have tried to clarify some of the important preoccupations of Raja Rao above, but here I want to unravel his method of reasoning and philosophizing.

Some clues are provided by the text. Siva is shown to be a mathematician in the book, but he hardly does any mathematics. True, there are references to Poincare, Pascal, Einstein, and above all to Ramanujan, and his goddess Namakkal, and a sprinkling of mathematical terminology throughout the book, but the fact is that Siva spends most of his time discussing philosophy with lovers, friends, and acquaintances. Raja Rao would imply that he is a mathematician not because he does mathematics, but because he uses a mathematical method to do philosophy. Siva explains his method somewhat like this:

> The fact is, like in any mathematical equation, you make a series of statements, and you reduce one to the other, till you get one clear class. As I was telling Michel ... the only equation that now remains and remains to be solved, is the hindu-hebraic one, the vertical or the horizontal, I repeat, the zero or the infinity, historylessness or Krishna or Moses.
> (260)

This method is found in its early stage in *The Serpent and the Rope* where Rama, the historian, spends most of his time in the same kind of discussions that Siva indulges in. As Savithri says of

Rama: "... he works with symbols and equations. History for him is a vast algebra, and he draws in unknowns from everywhere to explain it" (183).

Or as Rama says to himself: " And thus I tried to formulate myself to myself. I like these equations about myself or others, or about ideas: I feed on them" (195).

Similarly, Siva tries to find the equation or formula of ideas:

> ... in mathematics when you have a certain method to the solution of a problem ... you apply the same method to all sets of problems in the same series. Similarly, when you understand one fundamental principle in indian [sic] philosophy, you apply the same method of interpretation to every other problem in the same system, the same series. And I treat all indian mythology as a set of equations, and I apply my technique to it, and the results are astounding.
> (271)

Or to put it more pithily, this is Siva's "new doctrine of mathematics or philosophy" – "words are numbers and numbers words ..." (318). I would characterize Siva's method as a kind of reduction. The Latin root of reduce is *reducere*, "to lead back – *re* (back) + *ducere* (to lead), whose past participle is *ductus* (a leading, conducting), which gives us the modern word, "duct," hence "conduce" and "conduct." Among the meanings of "reduce," these apply to Raja Rao's method: "to put into a simpler or more concentrated form"; "to bring into a certain order; systematize"; and "to break up into constituent elements by analysis" (*Webster's New World Dictionary*). As Siva observes to Mireille at the beginning of the book,

> ... you know the secret of thought is in etymology, the secret of etymology in the root sounds, the bijaksaras, as the hindus call them, and these are like our integers, eternal figures of a cosmic computation, a sort of arithmetic of God. (33)

Raja Rao rightly calls his method "a doctrine" because we realize, when we read his books, that his method is far from "scientific" or "logical." This logic is all his own kind; everything must have "instantaneous meaning"; that is why Swanston, the Cambridge leftist intellectual tells Rama, "There are too many incomprehensible factors in your statement, sir," (*The Serpent and the Rope*: 182). Raja Rao's method of reduction is, therefore, more poetic than philosophical in the traditional sense of the word. The knowledge that this method produces is not knowledge in the strict sense of the term; it is more like a totalized realization. It is by employing this type of personalized, intuitional reduction that Siva comes to the conclusion that India represents the quest for zero, the vertical, the ahistorical and the abhuman, while the Judeo-Christian, Chinese, and Communist civilizations represent the quest for the infinite, the horizontal, the historical, the human: "Either you seek the Truth like Gandhi, or like Mao-Marx, create here on earth, the sino-judaic human empire" (145). Moreover, it is by this system that each character comes to represent some sort of abstraction, a formula – "What then is Jayalakshmi? A genetic formula. An equation that, like Ramanujan's, comes clearly from the Goddess" (131). Thus, relationships become equations – to be solved and resolved.

The third interpretative strategy that I find useful is to read the book against the grain. A beginning in this direction was suggested, as I mentioned earlier, by David McCutchion. Recently, Paul Sharrad has based his reading of *The Serpent and the Rope* on this principle. He refuses to accept the authority of Raja Rao and the power it confers on his male protagonists. Whereas other critics have been merely angry with Raja Rao or with his heroes for being poseurs, narcissists, or male chauvinists, Sharrad sees in these figures a tension between contradictory forces. He views the text as the battle ground for these forces. Instead of seeing the book as a coherent whole and seeing its characters as rounded personalities, Sharrad would like to see them as divided internally by the contradictions and tensions of the culture they try to portray:

> I shall be going on to argue that every culture is founded

> upon contradictions and tensions between constructed coherence (unity) and natural disorder (plurality). "... Rao's recourse to tradition, especially in a culture as complex as that of India, casts him into contradiction and plurality despite his quest for some unified, stable base, so that in *The Serpent and the Rope* he is paradoxically most Indian not because he upholds some "official" cultural standards, but because he dramatizes the inherent conflicts of his own and of any other culture. (16)

Raja Rao is, thus, seen as being Indian not because of, but in spite of, himself. Sharrad's book is a portion of his PhD dissertation, "Open Dialogue: Metropolitan-Provincial Tensions and the Quest for a Post-Colonial Culture in the Fiction of C J Koch, Raja Rao and Wilson Harris," at Flinders University of South Australia (1986). As such, the book contains a lot of dispensable background information and observations on both Raja Rao and his milieu. Moreover, Sharrad's interpretation is not based so much on changed notions of the nature of a text or of reading, but is grounded upon a certain view of postcolonial culture as a picture of conflict, not cohesion. He sees a homology between cultural conflict and textual conflict, between the contrary pulls of postcolonial India and of Rama. The conflict, again, is defined in terms of the commonplace tradition-modernity paradigm. Thus, Sharrad's method is a type of "vulgar" sociology of literature, which is both simplistic and unilinear in tracing the influence of culture on literature. Yet, it is a valuable beginning in a new direction. For nowhere in the criticism of Raja Rao do we find an analysis like the following:

> The fundamental lack of authenticity in Ramaswamy's "autobiography" derives from his attempt to play the roles of both victim and hero, provincial and metropolitan. He claims the mutually exclusive privileges of both roles – proclaiming the risks he takes while seeking protection, presenting himself as lover while revealing his incapacity for love, allying himself with figures of action but taking a

> passive stance in the face of events that might challenge his
> responsibility. (68)

Sharrad has thus shifted the ground from the similar "literary" analysis of McCutchion to cultural and ideological grounds. Here, I think, lies a great unexplored potential for rereading Raja Rao.

I would like to end this essay on *The Chessmaster* with a beginning in this direction. *The Chessmaster*, as I see it, is the most powerful attempt in contemporary English literature to temporize and legitimize an ideology that denies the ultimate reality of the phenomenal world. In doing this, Raja Rao is going against the dominant culture not only of the West where he has spent most of his life, but of today's India. This book defies the dominant culture not only in its content, but also in its form. It goes against the practices of the Western book trade with its cynical consumerism, cheap sales gimmicks, and corrupting system of incentives and threats. This is not the kind of book which will be promoted at black-tie cocktail parties or expensive publishers' bashes. This is an embarrassing book to have been written in the present world. Certainly, no "mainstream" author could have written such a book and found a publisher for it. It has no relevance to contemporary issues or to current publishing trends. It does not fit into any slot, not even into the slot of the great Indian English novel. It has not been written merely for the here and now, but for the hereafter.

Mulk Raj Anand once said to me about Raja Rao, "It's not enough to go on and on about Atman and Brahman, about the reality of Brahman and the illusion of the world; it won't do to cling blindly to Sankara's Advaita of the ninth century. Our problems are different. How do we solve them? Can Sankara's answers serve us today?" These were challenging questions for an admirer of Raja Rao to answer, so I kept quiet. But on reading *The Chessmaster*, I think I have found at least one way of answering them. Raja Rao does not deny the world or its suffering, brutality, and violence. His book is imbued with the very real problem of dukkha, the cosmic sorrow that Buddha sought to eliminate from the world. Raja Rao's book does turn a blind eye to history or its record of cruelty, to Birkenau and Buchenwald. He does not neglect politics, economics, or history. But to challenges that the human being faces anywhere – whether in Paris, London, or Calcutta, Raja Rao's answers point inward, from the exterior to the interior, from the outside to the inside, from the world to the self. Each one of us, he seems to say, must perform this little operation on ourselves – to dissolve ourselves into the nothing from which the whole world was created. To put an end to ourselves and thus to solve, once and for all, the problem of humanity. Deny yourself to become That. To me it is not this philosophy or its viability that are important, but the enormous energy and artistic integrity with which it is mediated through seven hundred pages of *The Chessmaster*. However difficult the philosophy may seem to some, the characters are real, their suffering is real, their concern with the human problem is real. It is clear to me that however tempted we may be to do so, we cannot dismiss this book or ignore it. That would only be to deny and repress what we don't find palatable in our present understanding of literature and of the world. Our rejection will tell us more about ourselves than about the book, just as our acceptance of the book tells us more about our predispositions than about the virtues of the text. The problems are our's, not the book's.

Anyhow, I would certainly not like to end this essay on a defensive note. I long to read *The Chessmaster* again, preferably after the next two volumes of the trilogy are out, to be back in the world of Raja Rao, to savour the sheer poetry of that world, its haunting ache, which I feel to the very marrow of the soul. Raja Rao's books, no doubt, are literary, but they take one to very fundamental function of the arts. As Sri Adwayananda reminds us in the transcription of his talks recorded at the National Centre for Performing Arts, Mumbai, the word for art is Kala in Sanskrit, Malayalam, and in many Indian languages – "'Ka' refers to Brahma. So, any art must take you Indian art, especially, takes you – to This. That is the real background of all the Indian arts" (3). Of all the contemporary novelists writing in English, I cannot think of anyone who has performed this pristine artistic role more sincerely, consistently, or successfully than Raja Rao. Raja Rao, as Braj B Kachru once told me, has invested the English language with the sacred thread, the yagnopavitam, which confers the twiceborn status to it. Of course, this sacralization must not be viewed in a casteist light, but as Raja Rao himself says in *The Chessmaster*, "Every man is twiceborn, a brahmin — the first when he's born to his mother, and the second when [he] is reborn, into himself, into his own knowledge of Self" (93). In Raja Rao's writing, the novel itself becomes twiceborn, first emerging from silence into language, and then, turning inward — making us, its readers, turn inward — returning itself, and us, to the silence beyond speech. To me, reading Raja Rao is a religious experience, and, from such a perspective, *The Chessmaster* is one of the most moving, in fact, one of the saddest stories I have read.

Notes

1. See my introduction to the Raja Rao Classic published by Katha (New Delhi: 1998). Also see an earlier version of this essay, "*The Chessmaster and His Moves*: A Review of Reviews and an Introduction" in *Comparative Perspectives on Indian Literature*. In an article in the *World Literature Today* number on Raja Rao (Autumn 1988) R Parthasarathy identifies other two parts of the trilogy as *The Daughter of the Mountain* and *A Myrobalan in the Palm of Your Hand* (561). These tentative titles have since been changed several times.

2. I have necessarily to be somewhat discreet about the identity of these critics because they know Raja Rao personally and would not like to be quoted. Raja Rao himself seems not displeased with the difficulty level of his book: "It is a very complex book. A lot of my friends said they found it impossible to read. R K Narayan said it went completely over his head." ("A Writer and his Moves" by Anuradha Chopra, *Times of India*, 29 October, 1989: 8).

3. McCutchion's article appeared first in the *Writers Workshop Miscellany*, no 8 (September-October 1961): 91-99. It was reprinted in his *Indian Writing in English: Critical Essays* (Calcutta: Writers Workshop, 1969): 69-82, and again in

Considerations. Ed Meenakshi Mukherjee (New Delhi: Allied, 1975): 90-101.
4. See, for instance, "What is the Third World Novel?" by Viney Kirpal in *The Journal of Commonwealth Literature*, 23.1 (1988): 145-156. I have discussed this issue in my paper, "The Ideology of Form: Notes on the Third World Novel," *Journal of Commonwealth Studies*, 25.1 (1991): 19-32.
5. For an introduction to Indian philosophy see P T Raju, *The Philosophical Traditions of India* (London: George, Allen and Unwin, 1971). For a more detailed exposition see, Surendranath Dasgupta, *The History of Indian Philosophy* 5 vols (1922; rpt Delhi: Motilal Banarsidas, 1988).

Works Cited

Adwayananda, Sri – Sri K Padmanabha Menon. *Atmaswarupam: One's Own Real Nature.* Malakara and Austin, TX: Advaita Publishers, 1988.

Atmananda, Sri. *Atmananda Tattwa Samhita: The Direct Approach to Truth as Expounded by Sri Atmananda – Sri Krishna Menon.* Ed Sri Adwayananda – Sri K Padmanabha Menon. Malakara and Austin, TX: Advaita Publishers, 1991.

Dasgupta, Surendranath. *The History of Indian Philosophy* I-V. 1922; rpt Delhi: Motilal Banarsidas, 1988.

Chopra, Anuradha. "A Writer and His Moves." The *Times of India,* (29 Oct 1989): 8.

Kirpal, Viney. "What is the Third World Novel?" *The Journal of Commonwealth Literature,* 23.1 (1988): 145-156.

McCutchion, David. "The Novel as Shastra." *Indian Writing in English: Critical Essays.* Calcutta: Writers Workshop, 1969: 69-82.

Paranjape, Makarand. "Introduction." *The Best of Raja Rao.* New Delhi: Katha, 1998.

—. The Chessmaster and his Moves: A Review of Reviews and an Introduction." *Comparative Perspectives on Indian Literature.* Ed A Ramakrishna Rao. New Delhi: Prestige Publications, 1992: 81-102.

—. "The Ideology of Form: Notes on the Third World Novel." *Journal of Commonwealth Studies,* 25.1 (1991): 19-32.

Raju, P T. *The Philosophical Traditions of India.* London: George, Allen and Unwin, 1971.

Rao, Raja. *The Cat and Shakespeare.* 1965; rpt New Delhi: Orient Paperbacks, 1971.

—. *The Chessmaster and His Moves.* New Delhi: Vision Books, 1988.

—. *The Serpent and the Rope.* 1960; rpt New Delhi: Orient Paperbacks, 1968.

Sharrad, Paul. *Raja Rao and Cultural Tradition.* New Delhi: Sterling, 1987.

World Literature Today. Autumn, 1988.

WINFRED P LEHMANN
RAJA RAO: MASTER OF LANGUAGE, RIGVEDA 10.81.7

As Raja Rao has informed us, he is a Brahmin of the Advaita school. By its tenets, the only reality is Brahman, and reality is undivided, Advaita; the world before our eyes is Maya, unreality. In this situation, what is the role of the writer? We may find the beginnings of an answer in Hymn 81 of the tenth book of the Rigveda. The hymn is addressed to Vishvakarman, creator of the world – literally, maker of everything. A short hymn consisting of only seven stanzas, it identifies the creator as a sacrificing priest, and goes on to ask,

> Where was the place, which was the primeval material, and of what kind, from which Vishvakarman created the world and disclosed the heavens in their greatness, he who is totally eye? (Rigveda, 10.81.6)

After expanding on the qualities of Vishvakarman and on the problem, the hymn goes on to exhort the listeners to contemplate the question. It concludes by addressing Vishvakarman with the title of this paper: Vacaspati, "master of language," and asks for his favour.

Through mastery of language, then, the world was created. Or to recall Raja Rao's straightforward statement in his address to the South Asian Language Association in 1984: "Vac created the world. Pure naming is pure creation." And from this he concludes: "Poetry now becomes the paradigm of the creator creating universes." That is to say, the writer or poet must set out to portray reality. In elaboration of this conclusion he goes on to comment on a longer and more explicit hymn on the creation of the world, the Purusha Sukta, or Hymn of Primal Man, which identifies the primeval material as a gigantic man who was sacrificed to create the world. In its sixteen verses this hymn, 10.89, lists created things, such as animals and classes of humans, also the verses, chants, and as Raja Rao puts it, the "sacrificial word," that is, the three older Vedas. He concludes: "the word then ended in pure meaning."

This concern with language, the elevation of the word as creative tool, contrasts sharply with the concern of authors in the Western tradition, as I have pointed out elsewhere (1995, 1996). Homer's concern in the Iliad is stated in the first word *menin*, wrath, the anger of Achilles and its consequences; in the Odyssey it is *andra*, a man – elaborated to a very clever man – who has many adventures. Goethe, in his major work, even has Faust dismissing the straightforward translation of *logos* as word in the Gospel of John, replacing it with "action." Dante may come closest to the Indian tradition with his treatise on the vernacular which he chose for the *Divine Comedy* rather than the traditional Latin. But none of the Western authors begins a major work with a statement like Kalidasa's in his *Raghuvamsa*, "Dynasty of Raghu," in which vac is the first word of the poem. Kalidasa then continues with a request for appropriate language, rather like Milton in *Paradise Lost* with a supplication to the heavenly muse that he might present adequately the account of "man's first disobedience" and its results. Like Rao, Kalidasa recognizes the poet as creator through control of language; in Ryder's translation the first words of the poem read:

> Like language and meaning tightly bound-

> to understand that language-meaning union
> I invoke Earth's parents, so too united,
> Parvati and the Supreme Lord.

Because of our differing views of language it is essential, for understanding the works of Raja Rao, also to understand the Indian treatment of language, a conclusion that is supported by the frequent mention in *The Chessmaster and His Moves* of the great Indian linguist, Panini. The esteem in which Panini is held may be exemplified by citing a passage that states the hero Sivarama's objective, "To find those fundamental arguments of thought, by which the language of mathematics could approach, say, the laws of Paninian grammar" (628). Those laws, or rules, produced by this remarkable linguist in the fifth century before our era, and elaborated by many later linguists, not least by Sumitra Katre in her superb edition, describe Sanskrit more fully than any other language that has been described. Moreover, the description has a totally different basis from ours – the basis from which Kalidasa and Rao produce their masterpieces.

To state the difference simply, we begin our concern with language from the bottom, the sound system, while the Indians begin from the top, the meaning. George Bernard Shaw has his *Pygmalion*, based on the great English linguist Sweet, setting out to raise Eliza from a flower-girl to a duchess through phonetics. More recently, we may begin from the sentence and its forms, as in Bloomfield's discussion of Jill getting an apple from Jack by saying "I want that apple." Or the analysis of the sentence may be more explicit syntactically, as when Chomsky breaks up his paradigm sentence: "The man hit the ball" into noun phrases, verb phrases and so on, continuing to turn his attention from the Transformational through the Government and Binding theory, thereupon the Principles and Parameters theory, and finally the Minimalist theory, to the virtual extinction of interest in linguistics except among the devotees. Among Western linguists, attention to meaning is subordinated, as in Bloomfield's dictum assigning meaning as the responsibility of all sciences. To illustrate the primacy of syntax, Chomsky devised sentences like: "Sincerity may admire the boy," a sentence that is syntactically correct but semantic nonsense.

In direct contrast to the Western view of language, the Indian begins with meaning. Any sentence is conceived at this level, and then filtered through three more before it is uttered. From the level of meaning, there is a progression through another level with a set of karaka categories, to a third set corresponding to actual sentences and forms, and finally to a fourth providing the actual expression, the concern in *Pygmalion*.

What has aroused the greatest comment on this approach to language is the level below that of the meaning with its karaka categories. We may note that the term is based on the same root, kar, as that in the name of Vishvakarman of Rigveda 10.81. In using language then, authors and other speakers are doers, makers, creators who set out to depict their perception of reality.

When they do so, the essential element of the sentence is taken to be the verb, of which there are two categories: kriya, translated as "act" or "performance," but more accurately "to be performed," and sadhya "to be attained, to be formed"; the two verb types correspond roughly to transitive and intransitive verbs. Other elements of the sentence, such as nouns, are conceived as standing in relation to the verb. There are six such relationships, or karaka categories. In the sentence, "Shakespeare wrote *Hamlet*," the element "Shakespeare" stands in kartr or "one who does or creates" relationship with the verb; "*Hamlet*" stands in karman or "what he does or creates" relationship. The four other karaka categories are karana, "doing with" or instrument relationship, adhikara, "placement" or locative relationship, sampradana, "act of giving" or dative, and apadana, "act of taking away" or ablative relationship.

Probably the central feature in achieving an understanding of this approach is a recognition of the Indian view that actions cannot be perceived, only their results can. Accordingly, in the process of formulating meaning, the author or speaker first employs a layer that relates the elements in an action or state to the action or state expressed by the verb. The layer below the meaning layer, the karaka layer, then consists of a set of situations.

Our view is totally different. We say that the verb "write" represents an action. In our view, it governs the object "*Hamlet*," in the sentence "Shakespeare wrote *Hamlet*." We state that Shakespeare was carrying on an activity that consisted of producing a literary work. Omitting a karaka layer, we see language as corresponding to the two further levels assumed by Indian linguists in the production of sentences. The third down is parallel to our grammar. But at this level the Indian grammarians do not refer to the basic form of nouns as representing a specific meaning, such as the nominative; rather, they label the cases by ordinal numerals such as the first, the second, third, and so on. As production of the sentence continues, the karaka relationship of any nouns in the sentence must be expressed in one of these. In our sentence, the word Shakespeare would be expressed in the first of the noun inflections; in a sentence like "the play was written by Shakespeare," Shakespeare would still stand in the kartr·relationship, but would be expressed by the third inflection. Similarly, in a phrase like "a Shakespearean essay," the prospective adjective would be labelled kartr at the karaka level, and at the third, formulated as an adjective. When Western grammarians produced their grammars of Sanskrit, the forms of nouns like devas, devam, devena and so on were named nominative, accusative, instrumental, and the approach of the Indian grammarians was effectively concealed. The second or karaka layer was disregarded, as was the analysis of the process from meaning to ultimate expression at the phonetic level.

Recently efforts have been made to relate the Indian approach to Chomskyan linguistics, as by Kiparsky and Staal. The karaka categories are equated to deep structure cases. But Kiparsky and Staal are troubled by the karaka relationships; these are specified more precisely, as in the production of compounds, where the relationships among the two elements in pot-maker, stalk-cutter, Veda-reader differ from one another.

They conclude that "Panini's treatment of syntax and semantics presents analogies to various aspects of several modern linguistic theories, without being directly identifiable with any of them" (1969:110).

Another effort relates Indian grammatical theory to that used in artificial intelligence. In an excellent article on "knowledge representation in Sanskrit and artificial intelligence," Briggs finds similarity in that both approaches start from meaning; because of this similarity, in his view "much work in AI has been reinventing a wheel millennia old" (1985:32). Besides likening the analysis of meaning in Indian grammar with the semantic nets proposed by specialists in artificial intelligence, Briggs sees an "important similarity between the two treatments of the sentence" in taking the verb as the focal point. He also credits the Indian approach as "more specific by rendering the activity as a 'going-event,' rather than 'going.'" By that approach, the process of a leaf falling from a tree is treated as "a uniting and disuniting of an agent" rather than "a change from one location to another." This treatment is "equivalent to the concept of addition to and deletion from sets." In addition to being more complete, Indian linguistics expresses "an event of 'moving' ... [as] at each instant, a disunion with a preceding point (the source, the initial state), and a union with the following point, toward the destination, the final state," ... "a calculus-like concept" (1985:39). Noting their failure in the attempt to depict meaning as such, the specialists in artificial intelligence might do well to adopt the approach of Panini and his successors by employing a karaka level.

The differing views of language in Western and Eastern tradition may be exemplified by some of the criticism of Raja Rao's writing. With our understanding of language we expect authors to depict action, to explicitly indicate change. In keeping with this view the critic Advani says of *The Serpent and the Rope*: "Never in the reviewer's range of reading has so little happened in so many pages." He characterizes the book as "a torrential burst of poetic power – a river on a furious rampage, spilling on all sides, with no single direction [so that] one's mind reels"

(Naik 112). Returning to Briggs's characterization of Indian linguistics, we understand the basis of Advani's objection; the novel presents a set of events rather than a series of actions. In his aim to depict reality, or the ultimate, Raja Rao writes at the karaka level. Advani's difficulty is all the more striking through his use of the phrases "torrential burst" and "furious rampage" in characterizing a book with the initial epigraph: "Waves are nothing but water, so is the sea."

Even McCutchion's review that Naik considers "one of the most perceptive" asks: "Is this a novel at all? ... All the central concerns of the Western novel are absent – social relations, psychological motivation ... judgment, a passion for the concrete" (104). The "calculus-like" progression in *The Serpent and the Rope* conceals for McCutchion the social and psychological forces that a Western novelist would provide through concrete depiction supported by judgmental comment. At the karaka level we find only states that reflect social order, situations that are the result of psychological motivations, individuals acting in accordance with their karma, which hardly allows judgment, and relationships that may lead to concrete actions.

In the preface to his book on Raja Rao, the eminent Indian critic, C D Narasimhaiah, credits him with "altering the expression to accommodate a distinct, profoundly Indian sensibility" besides "recapturing the magnificent mythical imagination of Indian antiquity" (xii). I have attempted to suggest some of the bases of that sensibility.

For the Advaita Brahmin Raja Rao, reality is a set of relationships and states. Accordingly, the acts of love in "The Goblets of Shiraz," the central section of *The Chessmaster and His Moves*, must, for example, be depicted as a set of relationships, rather than as romantic actions with the four women. Similarly, the shorter section of *The Cat and Shakespeare* in the brothel informs us of the social situation of the prostitute and of Nair's scarcely reputable behaviour as a ration clerk, rather than of amorous action. A contrast with Western tradition may be found in one of Comrade Kirillov's favourite authors, DH Lawrence, by scanning a few passages in *Lady Chatterley's Lover.*

As another example, for us the interaction between the Brahmin and the Rabbi in the third section of *The Chessmaster and His Moves* is undramatic; the utterances of each represent the relative views of Siva and Michel. Similarly, the episode dealing with the judge and Nair in *The Cat and Shakespeare* consists of a set of exchanges ending with the odd situation where the judge "went round and round the table looking at who?"

In the aim to portray reality or pure meaning the author must seek to write at the karaka level. Words then are mantras, not the phonetic, lexical items of a novel in the Western tradition. By recognizing the avenue to reality and the advantages of depicting it through use of language at the karaka level, we may come to understand more fully the art of Raja Rao.

Works Cited

Briggs, Rick. "Knowledge Representation in Sanskrit and Artificial Intelligence." *The AI Magazine* (Spring 1985): 32-39.

Katre, Sumitra M. *Astadhyayi of Panini.* Austin: The U of Texas P, 1987.

Kiparsky, Paul and J F Staal. "Syntactic and Semantic Relations in Panini." *Foundations of Language* 5 (1969): 83-117.

Lehmann, Winfred P. "The Yolk in the Pea-Hen's Egg: Language as the Ultimate Reality." *Literary India: Comparative Studies in Aesthetics, Colonialism, and Culture.* Ed Patrick Colm Hogan and Lalita Pandit. Albany: State U of New York P, 1995. 81-99.

—. "Poetic Principles in the South Asian Literary Tradition: Inter-relatedness of Grammar, Prosody and Other Elements of Language." *College Literature*, Special Issue. Ed Patrick Colm Hogan and Lalita Pandit (1996): 111-23.

Naik, M K. *Raja Rao.* New York: Twayne, 1972.

Narasimhaiah, C D. *Raja Rao.* New Delhi: Arnold-Heinemann, nd.

Rao, Raja. *The Serpent and the Rope.* New York: Pantheon, 1960.

—. *The Cat and Shakespeare: A Tale of Modern India.* New York: Macmillan, 1965.

—. *Comrade Kirillov.* New Delhi: Orient Paperbacks, 1976.

—. "The Ultimate Word." *Indian Horizons* 39.3-4 (1990): 7-17.
—. *The Chessmaster and His Moves.* New Delhi: Vision, 1988.
Ryder, Arthur W. *Kalidasa: Translations of Shakuntala and Other Works.* London: Dent (Everyman's Library 629), 1912.

RAMAN SRINIVASAN

BLINDING I: TOWARD A POETICS OF POST-TRADITIONAL TECHNOLOGY

"When you accept the object totally (square and whole, if you like) – you go beyond the object." – Raja Rao

Raja Rao can be read as both a writer of mantras and (therefore, of) manifestos. His now famous Foreword to *Kanthapura* is an early example of Raja Rao as a writer of revolutionary prose. Through seven decades of ardent practice, he has demonstrated an enduring commitment to nurturing a new sensibility in the English language. In addition, Raja Rao has also opened the doors for serious investigation into the nature of historiography, science, and technology from an Indian point of view.

I read *The Serpent and the Rope* as a challenge to the impoverished historiography of India. The more recent *Chessmaster* trilogy can be read as a sustained exploration of the notion of an "Indian science." Raja Rao's latest unpublished novel is yet again a highly original disquisition on the nature of technology. The protagonist of this most recent Raja Rao novel is an erudite Indian hydraulic engineer immersed in the world of mantra-shastra. In each of his novels, Raja Rao has thus created a serious and sustained intellectual dialogue between the classical and modern.

I was drawn to the work of Raja Rao during the course of my research in the history of Indian technology. In this essay, I submit some preliminary thoughts on a poetics of post-traditional technology. I am immeasurably indebted to Raja Rao for his generous comments and constant encouragement. Needless to say, I alone am responsible for all errors of interpretation, commission and omission.

The archaic is ever with us, outlasting you and me. Cattle rustlers use cellular phones in Nevada and pirates in the South China Sea navigate with hand-held GPS systems. The American soldier remembered "the skulking way of war" and so survived in Vietnam, and now thanks his Mashpee great-grandmother for advising him in dreams. On Labour day, you might light the charcoal fire with a high-tech lighter, but you still burn the raw meat just as your fathers have done for millenia. Archives disappear, nibbled away by white ants grown fat on greenbacks. History, too, is ephemeral unless the scribes sharpen their tusks and re-copy the palm leaves before the termites feast, but what endures is the archaic.[1]

The archaic endures naturally. Until a genocidal modernity comes along it is there somewhere, like the handwritten love letters from the first boyfriend or the ancient grandmother sitting in a corner twirling her beads; it is there somewhere, like the Raj hobbling along on prosthetic feet. Yet we embrace the shining myth of the modern. Once we celebrate the "Modern," the postmodern has to be invented in a desperate Oedipal hurry, and New Worlds savaged totally.

Consider instead, one of Fredric Jameson's many definitions of postmodernism as a point of departure, and let us imagine post-traditionalism as what is when modernization cannot be completed and nature and culture are nearly gone for good. Tibetan monks in exile develop screen saver programmes based on Yantras for the IBM art gallery on Madison Avenue. That is the sort of tragedy and irony most of humanity faces today. Post-traditionalism is postmodernism that cares not to theorize and dares not learn from Las Vegas. Let a casino in, and Bingo! the whole reservation goes. Since decolonization, the whole world has become an empire of chance. Nothing is sacred to the greenback, not even the Sipapuni, not even Pashupatinath. In any case, how many Hoover Dams can one build to light up the night when cloud seeding technology is so primitive?[2]

Fredric Jameson, pre-eminent theorist of the postmodern, has argued that the modern is itself characterized by incomplete modernization and postmodernism is thus more modern than modernism itself. But, have you ever wondered, what results when modernization runs out of steam? The forests are all gone, and with the jungles, the angels and demi-gods of the woods also vanish, and all that is left, as Gadgil and Guha have pointed out, is "this fissured land."[3]

All that is left then, if one is lucky and anamnestic, is the memory of memory — of tigers and elephants, of bejewelled howdahs and mustachioed mahouts processioning through flower-strewn streets, to the accompaniment of fife and drum, serpent, clarinet and cymbals. To remember that memory of fragile memory, you may have to pack yogurt-rice and pickle in aluminium foil and travel to the archives and zoos in Washington DC, or the museums in Cleveland or Newark, New Jersey. Or petition Senator Inoue to sponsor another bill on the Hill.[4]

Do amputated limbs, supposedly gathered for a postmodern physical anthropology museum by a curious curator, have rights to cremation or burial or repatriation? Will such claims impede the march of science? Or will looking at the feet lead you to liberation? Supposedly a scientific understanding of traumatic injuries would benefit millions of people in Third World cities. We know, for instance, that powerful automobiles have been let loose on inadequate Indian roadways resulting in many gory accidents. Emergency medical care is non-existent on Indian highways and when available in cities, is woefully minimal. Thus sepsis remains a common problem arising out of a frustrating failure to maintain sterile operating theatres. In turn, it leads to numerous amputations in India.

Similarly, the inability to maintain a chain of cold refrigerators to keep polio vaccines potent, results in an inordinate number of polio victims in India even today. Both with amputees and polio patients, the obvious solution of wheelchairs for restoring mobility does not prove feasible in India; the simple reason being the relative rarity of plain paved surfaces taken for granted in the industrialized world. In the absence of rigid and smooth surfaces, a wheeled vehicle proves mostly a nuisance. Please question your veterans from Desert Storm. On the contrary, a simple walking stick, snapped off a tree, is often both an elegant and efficient solution for enhancing mobility. If one were rich, the camel and elephant would wait.

In fact, as William McNeil has pointed out in a brilliant essay, it is the "eccentricity of the wheel" as a technological innovation that needs explication through most of human history. Arguably, the wheeled cart is the pre-eminent vehicle of modernization and modernity. Hugh Kenner and other scholars have shown, for instance, that the automobile is intimately associated with the rise of high modernism.[5]

In the absence of a wheelchair, that other symbol of modernity, which will function satisfactorily, say, in Kabul or Khartoum, what can one do? Fund the MSF – the frontiersmen and women of modern medicine? Or stop exporting hand grenades, mines, explosives, automobiles, and wars? If that threatens to cause a global recession, perhaps one can at least not patent a cheap foot prosthesis. But who will invent an affordable prosthetic device and not patent it? How will it be made and marketed? Will the NIH let it go unpatented?

When the seer and seen merge with seeing, creation emerges, and meaning means "the face without face": thus Magritte's self-portrait, an illuminating illumination of the blinding I. The I of pure creativity, the I of pure poetry, of which the Vedic sages spoke with such intimacy, is what is "when time and place are burnt to ash ... (and) only light shines over." It is the "*moi pur*, the pronoun of universality," of Valéry. Mallarmé, *le Maitre* of Valéry, saw it as a terrifying Nothingness (and then the

Venetian mirror had to reflect for him, Stephane Mallarmé). "And after I found Nothingness," he wrote in 1866, "I found Beauty." That I, the faceless face of truth, impersonal and universal, according to the Indian tradition, is the very essence of knowledge, the light of light, the source of all creativity, be it literary or technological, and it is of the nature of the vak, vocable, word, the sabda. Whence did that I, "like the sea without the slightest ripple on its surface," come to be I? Whence did the rivers merge into the ocean?[6]

According to the Brahadaranyaka Upanishad, "In the beginning there was only the self. Looking around it saw nothing else than the self. It first said 'I am.' Therefore arose the name I."

Each and every word is a name that arises from the primal name. Therefore, to name correctly is to create, poetically that is. And to name, one must be truly anonymous, for the hidden names will not reveal themselves to the self-conscious. The name Kalidasa, you will find nowhere, in his entire corpus, for how can he who is docile around Kali claim authorship? Therefore inventing and naming are related activities. Thus it is that poetry is a paradigm of creation in Indian cosmology, and the Vedic seers and poets compare themselves to artificers.

"The idea, entirely unfamiliar to the modern world, that nature and language are inwardly akin, was for ages well known to various high cultures whose historical continuity on the earth has been enormously longer than that of Western European culture," observed Benjamin Lee Whorf, celebrated linguist and accomplished engineer. He was interested in Indic thought and at the suggestion of a fellow student of Indian philosophy, Fritz Kunz, published the essay, "Language, Mind, and Reality." In it he made a bold connection between technological design and linguistics, paving the way for an aesthetics of technology. "We do not think of the designing of a radio station or a power plant as a linguistic process," he wrote, "but it is one nonetheless." His insights into the connectedness of nature and language, of words and things, and machine and mantra suggest a poetics of technology. From an Indic perspective, the mantra is the machine par excellence, and language itself, a primal technological system. (Learning to use a machine, as you know, is not unlike learning a new language.)[7]

Whorf was one of the earliest, in the West, to recognize the creative dimension of sound and language, an idea appreciated in India through the mantram. What is mantra or mantram? Simply put, mantram is a phonic device to aid cognition. It can be apparently meaningless syllables, or words and phrases. The correct enunciation of these sonic devices produces various kinds of results. Phrases, such as "I love you," or "God Bless America," are but crude mantras.

Mantras are sometimes uttered to be heard, as in "I love you," but the more potent a practitioner is, the less the need to audibly sound the sabda, the word.

> Mantras are a form of speech ... oriented toward the very origin of the word and of the energy. Therefore instead of activating the ordinary mental process and drawing their utterer toward the world of differentiation, the mantra makes the user turn within, toward the primary, transcendental, source of all speech, and therefore of all manifestation.

The sabda, the ultimate word, is thus the basis of all creativity. It is the very essence of reality, of what Rilke adores as "*du bist Gross*," of what the Upanishads call Brahman. "The word is the very essence," says Bhartrhari (5th century CE), the great linguist, "of all objects, and creation. It is indestructible, the aksaram, the phoneme."

By naming the proper name, the cosmologically correct name, the thing is perceived to be. But names are hidden, and only the Seer sees them. As the French sage Paul Valéry reported, "objects come to be named." In an essay on Indian poetics, Raja Rao has written,

> Suppose then, the yogi modulates his breath with such strictness, precision, as the word would say itself to itself totally – such a vibration then be its true, whole name. Imagine then, sitting by some Mount Meru, in the

> Manasarovar of my mind, I vibrate ... the vibration of the object, would not the object appear and say: Look, here I am.

Is that why our febrile yogis and ascetics are always chanting or regulating their breath, the prana? But why are the kings and prime ministers prone to speechifying?[8]

Speech involves modulation of the breath. To regulate the breath is to regulate the mind. You can test it yourself. Patanjali has stated it succinctly in the Yoga Sutras: "Disease, languor, indecision, carelessness, sloth, sensuality, misapprehensions, etc can be prevented by ... the expulsion and retention of breath." By adopting one of these methods, the many modifications of the mind, perturbations of perception are brought to a stand still. One breathes easily, regularly, and slowly and the eyes rest easily on the object. When one breathes in such a manner one's enunciation is precise, naming is spontaneous, and perception is clear. "Names are made of phonemes, graphics of breath." Then naming is creation by the anonymous. That is mantra-yoga. But who hears the mantra?

In the Brahadaranyaka Upanishad it is also said, "By the mind alone one sees, by the mind one hears." By way of exegesis, the sage Sankara has said,

> Just as an accomplished goldsmith can tell you the weight of an ornament without using any scales, there is the possibility of the mind perceiving an object, through its own great purity, even without calling on the aid of senses like the eye.

But then, Sir, who sees the mind seeing?[9]

Elmer Sperry, American inventor of many a practical device such as the gyroscopic aircraft controller, was often known to suddenly "pick up a pad and hold it at arm's length, then with a pencil in the other hand ... draw." A puzzled colleague once made bold to ask him about it. Sperry replied, "It's there! Don't you see it! Just draw a line around what you see." The colleague recalled that Sperry saw his inventions in the air and that "Whatever he saw, he saw a 100% perfect." Who saw?[10]

Thomas Hughes, historian of technology and biographer of Elmer Sperry, says that Elmer Sperry and other American inventors shared an ability to visualize entire machines, and systems in operation. Eugene Ferguson, distinguished engineering historian, in his critically acclaimed work, *Engineering and the Mind's Eye*, informs us that "pyramids, cathedrals, and rockets exist not because of geometry, theory of structures, or thermodynamics, but because they were first pictures – literally visions – in the minds of those who conceived them." Many inventors run physically unbuilt machines in their heads, checking it for problems. James Nasmyth, an English inventor, said that the machine "was in my mind's eye (as if ... in absolute material form and action) long before I saw it in action."

Imaginative engineers possess an almost mystical gift, an extraordinary degree of ability to run complex simulations in their minds. Convincingly demonstrating the extensive employment of the mind's eye in invention, Ferguson describes it as "the organ in which a lifetime of sensory information – visual, tactile, muscular, visceral, aural, olfactory, and gustatory – is stored, interconnected, and interrelated." The mind's eye is "the arbiter of all these (sensual) experiences ... Through it, we make sense of the physical world we inhabit." Ferguson further suggests that it is the mind's eye that enables us, for example, to "see a piece of cloth lying on a chair," and "say without touching it that it is probably soft (or harsh), pliable (or stiff), and a good (or poor) insulator against cold." What enables these inventors and engineers to see and feel non-existent things in their mind in so real a fashion? Is it akin to the process by which Indian seers saw the poems, and other things?

The mind's eye is sometimes called the eye of the gods in Indic traditions. Those blessed with it see words and things with their eyes shut. In ancient Sanskrit treastises on architecture, for example, the architect is required to travel, through his mind, to the world of gods to see their cities and copy them on their return to the world of humans. The ability to see through the mind's eye is also one of the rewards assured to practioners of yoga. Patanjali himself says so: "Then come quickness of mind, uninstrumental perception and mastery over the ab-original cause."

What is this creative intuition? From where does it arise? According to Whorf,

> ... the forms of a person's thoughts are controlled by inexorable laws of pattern, of which he is unconscious. These patterns are the unperceived intricate systematizations of his own language ... Every language is a vast pattern-system, different from others, in which are culturally ordained the forms and categories by which the personality not only communicates, but also analyzes nature ... and builds the house of his consciousness.

We all are imprisoned within our own house of consciousness and creativity is the ability to walk out of that house into consciousness itself. It is like stepping out to breathe fresh air in mid-winter.[11]

Whorf translates the word, "language" into the Sanskrit manas, often inadequately understood as the Mind. (Although the Mind's eye is translated as the eye of manas as well).

> Manas in a broad sense is a major hierarchical grade in the world-structure – a 'manasic plane' as it is indeed explicitly called ... (and) in the plane of the Manas there are two great levels, called the rupa and arupa levels,

explains Whorf. Rupa is the level of the concrete manifestation and arupa is the level of the abstract and unmanifest. The level of the manifest is binomial, that of nama-rupa, name and form. The name is heard through the ear and the form seen through the eye, and what differentiates name and form are just the differing instruments needed for their perception. At the higher level of arupam, the unmanifest, they are aspects of one and the same.[12]

How can one open the Third eye, the Mind's eye? How does one let the unmanifested Manasic plane inform the intellectual or the physical levels? "By doing tapasya" explained Masterji Ramachandra Sharma of Jaipur, the maker of the Jaipur Foot. As children, we had always heard stories of daemonic kings and daemonic sages engaging in arduous tapasya for many aeons, in order to obtain various goods and gods. So when I heard Masterji talk of doing tapasya, my mind ran movies of bearded ascetics standing still, with one leg wrapped around the other, hands held high, creepers entwining the torso, and anthills growing at the ankle. Masterji saw me see my movie and commented, "It does not mean just chanting sonorous chants of mystical syllables in some jungle or growing a beard and wearing khadi. Although chanting or regulating your breath does help calm the mind and make it receptive to creative ideas. It is an incandescent *askesis*.

"Tapasya, as you know, is a discipline, a fervent and earnest practice of one's duty," he told me in Bundelkhand. "It is an incubation, a fermentation, a germination of one's potentialities. It takes courage, dedication, perseverance, and discipline. It is one-pointedness in one's activities. For ultimately yoga is but skill in action, it is said."

Tapasya or tapas

> ... is precisely Hebrew Zimzum. Tapas is not a penance, because it is not expiatory, but rather an anguish and a passion: a dark heat of the consciousness, a kindling not yet a flame ... a smouldering continence and intellectual fermentation, as well as ... a vegetative incubation

wrote Ananda Coomaraswamy. It is an activity pregnant with contradictory dualities that opens up creative spaces, and febrile fields. "Masterji, when he is absorbed in a problem, neither eats nor sleeps, he does not even chew pan. His beard grows, making him look very much a yogi doing tapasya," a worker at the Jaipur Foot facility recalled.

The Indian Space Research Organization was also involved in an extended exercise of ardent devotion called SITE. Hundreds of engineers spent a year and a half trekking to the remotest villages in India to set up a satellite TV system. They travelled in drenching rain and piercing heat to keep the system working through the year in five thousand villages. Their dedication inspired and motivated thousands of other development workers throughout the country. It even enabled journalists, especially Western reporters, to see something positive about India for the first time. Out of this fervent tapasya by young teams of space engineers emerged a unique design for INSAT. It is even said that a significant number of talented ISRO engineers once threatened to stop work on the INSAT if it were not designed to cater to rural development. Such was the imprint of their year long exertion in the villages, that INSAT conjugated rural and urban interests in an unusually creative fashion, a bahuvrihi samasa of Sanskrit grammar applied to technological systems design. The symphony and synergy of its form and function made it more than a moral statement of a few radical engineers. Verily, INSAT rose heavenwards, a poetic chant.

Morality is the grammar of life and yoga, its poetics. By yoga, I mean more than the complex physical contortions that some are wont to identify as yoga, especially in America. Yoga is nothing less than the means of yoking the subject and object, declare the ancient texts. When the subject merges with the object, then it is pure delight, the gods in you are awakened. Create, is what the gods do. They maintain and destroy too. But even sustenance and destruction require the gods to be creative. Recall the terribly elegant descent of Narasimha, half-lion and half-man, in the legends: it is but one example of an innovative solution to an insoluble problem.

Conversely, and maybe more correctly, it is better to say that creativity is itself represented by gods in the Indic pantheon. After all, it is "from the human mind that the gods received their gift of creation." What Eugene Ferguson calls the mind's eye is also the gods' eye in Indic traditions. Thus the one question facing the artist, performer, engineer, poet or craftsman is: "How indeed to cease becoming and be instead but a vehicle of creativity?" What disciplines are adopted, and what attitudes are affected, in Indic civilization to ground the lightning – like intuition, to harness the creative impulse? How is it done? What is the method of Ramanujam?[13]

Ananda Coomaraswamy, Heinrich Zimmer, and Stella Kramrisch, three of the greatest Indologists, have addressed this question in their unsurpassed scholarship on Indian arts and crafts. It is beyond my capacity to summarize the work of these three unusually fecund scholars but what is clear from their work and life is the Indic notion that creativity arises from going inwards into the "space within the heart." Anything one desires can be fashioned from the lots of the heart, which is everywhere. According to Coomaraswamy, the idea of intellectual property rights is absurd. Ideas can only be entertained for they are gifts of the Spirit. Then the question is how does one learn to entertain ideas, receive guests and their gifts?

Nobility in receiving is as important as charity in giving. LBJ and John Foster Dulles never understood that. "We must not conclude," writes Coomaraswamy,

> ... that the artist is a passive instrument like a stenographer. "He" is much rather actively and consciously making use of "himself" as an instrument. Body and mind are not the man, but only his instrument and vehicle ... Inspiration and aspiration are not exclusive alternatives, but one and the same.

The artist/inventor has to be both contemplative and a good workman. By working toward progressive self-noughting, the necessary nobility for receiving the gift of the creative gods is nurtured.[14]

The Aranmula mirror, it is said, came as a gift of the god of Aranmula, Krishna, in a dream to an old woman of the Aachaari caste. Gods and gurus impart wisdom through subtle means implicitly and tacitly, rather than explicitly (as academics are wont to expect). Dreams, stories, jokes, songs, "incidents," unseen glances, and delectable eatables are all ways of instruction in the Indic world. After all, it is the heart that is to be detoxicated. According to local memory, the Raja of Tiruvalla had invited a group of metal-workers from Tamil Nadu to settle in Aranmula. The Tamilians, being Tamilians, accepted the king's generous hospitality and lazed about. The king's gold and copper they took and spent on wine and women. However, being silver-tongued by nature, they kept the king waiting for a long, long time saying this first and that later. Finally one day, the king lost his patience and demanded results. Unless the Tamil Aachaaris showed him something unique and laudable in craftsmanship, they would be severely punished. They thought and thought. "Now, we really have to produce something never seen before, so the Raja may be pacified." They scratched their heads in the heat of intense speculation.

One night, in an old woman's dream, the god of the temple, Lord Krishna himself appeared and ordered the womenfolk of the Aachaaris to throw their silvery tin bangles into the furnace. The women followed the instructions zealously and threw their bangles into the crucible used for melting copper. When the molten metal was poured anew into the mould, the old woman said, "Now, remove it carefully, and polish it slowly." The men did so and to their amazement, they had made a most wonderful shining mirror. They took it to the Raja who was immensely pleased and offered the mirror, verily the first Aranmula mirror, to Krishna, where you might still see it, way in the back of the sanctum sanctorum, in the ab-original shrine. That is how the Aranmula Mirror came to be.

"What about the more recent innovations you have made, Sir?"

Arjunan Aachaari looked at me quizzically. He had eliminated the need for a wax-pattern in the flask mould previously used to make the mirror. Instead, he placed three small chips of an older mirror on the periphery of the two face-plates of the mould, in effect eliminating several energy-consuming steps. He had converted, to put it simply, a lost-wax process into a die-casting process. "How did you get that idea?"

"When I am polishing well, my hands stop moving, or at least that is how it feels because my mind stops thinking; then I see things as if I were looking, at noon, down a well, and can see the patinating bronze pot that fell off the rope months ago. I have not really done much. Sometimes somebody will come to me with a broken part for making a spare for a foreign car or something. Then I look at it, and when I am polishing I will know how to do it. It may take a few weeks but sometimes they are in a hurry. What can I do? I am not well-educated."

Masterji in explaining the genesis of the Jaipur Foot says: "I was asked to make a foot that looked like a foot. That is all. Professor Sethi was generous enough to explain to me the principles of biomechanics. Then we tried to make a foot that looked like a foot. I am an artist and to make something life-like is my business. I had to give form, Rupa, to what I saw in mind. To do that I had to let my hands work and make sure my stupid ego does not interfere."

"The ego is the only enemy," Raja Rao has often warned me. Anonymity vanquishes the ego. It aims at liberation from the delusions of agency, of "I am the doer," of what is called asmita, I am-ness. It aims at detachment and at minimizing undue identification with the results of work. "I" am, in fact, not the doer, but the instrument. Thus the goal is not so much to distinguish onself, as to extinguish the self and be One with the world. The Gita's oft-quoted verse "There are rights only to work, not to the fruits," sums up the attitude of the serious artist, emphasizes the same approach. It is the gratification of the ten-headed monster, ego, that causes disaster. "The artist becomes a mere craftsman once the ego infects the work, making it less than universal. Once the ego is welcomed into the work, it is very hard to exterminate it. You kill it once here, and it sprouts there even before you know it, like a veritable Ravana. See what happened to this whole thing after all the awards and recognition. People thought they, as individual personalities, were being rewarded. All work stopped. No two colleagues remained friends. Total disaster. Tell that to your Rockefeller Brothers when you go back to New York. They can keep their awards," said a friend of the Jaipur Foot. He, a very wise and gentle man, prefers to remain free of the burdens of name and fame. True art and sincere artists remain anonymous, that is our belief in India. What is not anonymous is not art, just rows of empty Campbell soupcans.

Technology, undoubtedly, is an artful enterprise. Aesthesis, sensual knowledge, informs it as much as abstract knowledge. Delight, in the original sense of the word, is an integral savour (rasa in Sanskrit poetics) of technological practice. Some engineers, some artisans, are more graceful than others and some technological systems are more pleasing than others. Even the very first atom bomb provoked an aesthetic reaction, an aesthetics of horror, maybe. Elegance is, therefore, an essential and universal component of proper engineering design. The AK-47 is elegant when compared to say, a M-16. A Davy Crocket is held to be infinitely sexier than the Fat Man by nuclear weapons designers. Sub-critical tests conducted with teraflop machines are even more elegant. Less maniacal American inventors continue to come up with ever more pleasing devices for implementing the death penalty. Ultimately, whether any of them is any less messy than the royal punitive elephant is debatable. Nevertheless, we do, quite easily, recognize some computer programmes to be inherently more satisfying than others. Some bridges span shores more naturally than others, making us like, say, the work of Robert Maillart more than that of Robert Moses. Masterji rightly thinks of himself as an artist.

What constitutes beauty in technological artifacts, be they the merest shards of pottery from the Indus valley or the serpentine Interstates in San Fernando valley? How do engineering design and workmanship contribute to aesthetic delight and, conversely, how does an artistic sensibility, a sense of poesy, inform technological practice? How do aesthetic sensitivity and pragmatic logic interact in the world of the engineer or artisan? What enables the truly great engineer to make the concrete elegant, and thus remind us that real pragmatism is always graceful, a blessing in beauty? Philosophers have noticed that pragmatism, to be truly pragmatic, has to be poetic. Unless the practical is simultaneously aesthetic, civilization cannot endure. Conversely, if art is not integrated into the products and procedures of daily life, living becomes a struggle, a stress. This is what the history of classical civilizations teaches us. Coomaraswamy never tired of reminding us of Ruskin's warning, "Industry without art is brutality." How can technology be not only politically correct but also cosmologically correct? How can it make living not just comfortable but also graceful?

Like Coomaraswamy and Kramrisch, Heinrich Zimmer has also emphasized the metaphysical underpinnings of Indian artisanship. In his path-breaking work on Indian art, *Artistic Form and Yoga in the Sacred Images of India*, Zimmer has recognized an important feature of Indian material culture that material fabrications, by being artistic products, are designed to lead the user inwards, to be yogic in effect. The Indic sacred image, which Zimmer wrote about with unsurpassed understanding, is an excellent example of technological and artistic products whose main purpose is to show the user an inner tranquillity. But then the sacred image is just a reminder to one that everything is a sacred object. Kramrisch has pointed out that the object in India is known to exist at three levels, the physical, the psychological, and the metaphysical. And as Raja Rao has said, "When you accept the object totally (square and whole, if you like) — you go beyond the object. When you are in time totally, you go beyond time. That is creativity, that is prayer." When the object is viewed metaphysically, it is darshan, prayer. The old man making his staff in Thoreau's *Walden* is in deep prayer. Technology, if cosmologically correct, is imbued with a state of grace and is in turn, capable of transmitting ontological elegance. If incorrect, then like Oppenheimer, we too shall bemoan soiled hands.

Western history of the last two hundred years has proved that a physically comfortable, well-appointed environment can be produced using industrial technology. Is that sufficient? If it is, what are you going to do, Madam, with all those toxins that have been released in the last two hundred years? Ship it in pariah barges to unsuspecting shores?

David Pye in his brilliant and brief treatises on the nature and art of workmanship argues that a wide range of qualities in workmanship is necessary to give beauty and grace to our manufactured environment. The kinds of workmanship utilized in industrial mass production provide little room for variations in texture, finish, depth, overtone or subtlety of the objects because they are based on the workmanship of certainty. Witness the horrible limitations of workmanship of certainty in an industrially made prosthesis. Industrially produced environments, by limiting the range of qualities in objects, are akin to mono-cultural plantations in the tropics, commercially attractive but little else. Furthermore, by minimizing the workmanship of risk, industrial ecology permits little scope for either the artisan or the user to "totally accept the object and to be in time completely." The workmanship of certainty reduces rasa, sensual delight, in the material world, degrading the erotic to the pornographic. That degradation is inevitable if one does not intimately know the enjoyer, the seer who sees.[15]

Pye also usefully distinguishes between design and workmanship. "Design is what, for practical purposes, can be conveyed in words and by drawing: workmanship is what, for practical purposes, can not," he writes with characteristic precision. If design can be conveyed by words, do we not have to understand how words convey meaning? Raja Rao often asks, "Where does the word end and meaning begin?" "Where does the word end and the thing begin?" We may ask by analogy, "how can form and function be separated in machine design?"

Although design is expressible through words and pictures, workmanship is not. It is ineffable, being nirvacya, it has a subjective aspect to it. It is in the nature of ineffable, apophatic knowledge, that the individual is the king, even if he be but a lowly cobbler; it is the natural domain of the poet. How are workmen nurtured? The history of the industrial revolution, if one remembers it right, is a story of how workmanship was terminated, not created.

Engineering education in India, largely literary and mathematical in its approach, and taught in English rather than local languages, teaches, at best, design. Professor P K Sethi encountered this problematic facet of Indian engineering when trying to develop the Jaipur Foot and has lamented the unwillingness of Indian engineering to step out of its textual threshold. How does anything get done in India? Largely by non-literate, but highly skilled workers. Workmanship, so to speak, like sex education or metaphysics, is picked up on the streets. The one who is a serious student, say like Masterji, of course, finds a teacher and persuades him or her to impart ineffable knowledge. The challenge then, that the Indian engineer faces, is to design in a way that is consonant with the culture of the worker.

The Jaipur Foot evolved successfully precisely because Professor Sethi was willing to share the process of designing a prosthesis with Masterji and other workers. Masterji, in turn, was able to listen to the users of the prosthesis, for the user of a machine is an important worker in the process. On the other hand, although Professor M N Natarajan, in Chennai, could specify a design for a prosthesis not too different from the Jaipur Foot, he could not successfully produce one due to the lack of supportive and creative workmen. The design of INSAT too, involved active education and participation on the part of prospective users. INSAT's multi-purpose payload grew out of a commitment to listen to diverse user groups. However the ability to listen to users is not a sufficient guide for machine design. Arguably, INSAT's multiple payloads imposed the worst design criteria of each payload on the satellite and demanded a high degree of skill on the part of the workers who made the satellite. The design left little room for poor workmanship. All failures in INSAT have been conclusively traced to defective workmanship. It reflects poorly on the ability of designers to factor in the quality of workers. Engineers in Bangalore were not aware of the Californian work culture. What is worth emphasizing about INSAT is that the work of designing it was an exemplary workmanship of risk. That almost no other satellite involved such a challenging combination of missions and technologies, is acknowledged widely in the satellite industry.

The phenomenal success of the Jaipur Foot is, at some level, attributed to the tolerance of the design for varying levels of workmanship. The design is also quite forgiving of variations in material standards. The recipe for making the Jaipur Foot is like many a recipe used in the Indian kitchen, forgiving and tolerant of imprecision. The prosthesis is designed not to demand precision, either from the designer, the worker, the environment, or the user. Even the most skilled part of the process, that of making the die for the foot, is, although a highly skilled task, tolerant of imprecision. Tolerance, Abhinavagupta (the theorist of rasa, flavour in Indian poetics) might say, is the savour of the Jaipur Foot.

Tolerance in technological systems is driven out by mechanization and its accompaniment, standardization. Tolerant engineering design is possible only if a workmanship of risk is available. Tolerance in engineering design is a way of keeping the door open to individuality. Modernism in engineering cannot tolerate such tolerance. The house is a machine to live in, said Le Corbusier. In that respect, the modern is a fanatical fundamentalist that demands absolute obedience to the book, the book of standards and specifications. The engineering drawing is its Bible and quality control engineers are its Ayatollah Khomeinis, defining quality as narrowly as fundamentalists define religion. When tolerance is ruled out, with it goes individuality, diversity, art, and grace.

Intolerant engineering results in the loss of creative leisure and pleasure. Coomaraswamy could not emphasize enough Ruskin's prophetic observation, "Industry without art is brutality," adding to it the warning that if India were to industrialize, it too would become a nation of Shudras, workers, "industrious and ignorant" at once. People find little time to play and the *Journal of the American Medical Association* publishes research showing rates of depression have increased unmistakeably with modernization all over the world. So stock prices of satellite TV companies go up and they broadcast gleefully,

"The revolution will not be televised, my brother!"

Is creative work, artistic work, satisfying and elevating work not possible in a mechanized, industrialized world? Once again Pye's work provides a clarifying vocabulary. What people like Coomaraswamy, Kramrisch, Ruskin, and Gandhiji opposed was the termination of a spiritually elevating "workmanship of risk." According to Pye, where the quality of the result is predetermined before the work begins and cannot be altered once it has begun it is the workmanship of certainty. Modern printing, he says, involves the workmanship of certainty whereas writing with a pen is an example of the workmanship of risk. "A workmanship of risk ... [provides] an immensely various range of qualities" which is absolutely essential for a rich sensual environment. A workmanship of risk is, it turns out, essential not just for humans, but also for the more intelligent animals. Elephants, apes, monkeys, and dolphins develop serious behavioural problems in environments which do not let them engage in some form of workmanship of risk. American zoo keepers now engage behaviour enrichment consultants to keep the animals spiritually alive.

Thus the challenge for post-traditional technology is to create and sustain a material environment that is aesthetically pleasing and economically viable. If, as Benjamin Whorf pointed out, technological design is at its core a linguistic process, then the task for the post-traditional engineer is to construct not only a grammatically correct but also a poetically inspired material culture. Sanskrit, meaning well-constructed, is one of two classical languages of India. It is also an artificial language constructed with a formal and elaborate grammar. It, in a certain sense, provides a metaphor for post-traditional engineering. Sensitive to context, gender, number, environment, and amenable to creative manipulation, yet capable of precision and growth, Sanskrit seems to provide a model for thinking about technology in post-traditional India.

I must point out that post-traditional technology or culture is not the exclusive possession of India. In fact, it is a wide-spread phenomenon. Gregg Clancy's work on carpentry in the United States is a study of post-traditionalism in the American context. He has found that wood is not easily subject to the workmanship of certainty, and has so remained in the province of the workmanship of risk, and thus changed with time without ever being completely "modernized."[16]

Wood, being archaic and organic, is very resistant to modernization. In the context of materials engineering, modernization means standardization. Wood is too heterogenous to succumb to the standardizing imperative of modern engineering handbooks. Eric Schatzberg in his work on the wooden aeroplane shows how the inability of engineers to modernize wood resulted in their abandoning wood and instead adopting a more unsatisfactory and, at times, a more dangerous material, metal.

Metal, concrete, and plastic are perfect materials for the modern engineer. Modernism in architecture relies on metal and concrete because these materials enable the architect to usurp all control over workmanship. Concrete, steel, and glass are industrial materials par excellence and hence ideally suited to express modernism. Being industrial, they are also able to sustain the speed and intensity of modernist capitalism. Patrick Geddes, one of the earliest of the post-traditionalists, of course, recognized this years ago. Lewis Mumford's classification of technological history into paleotechnic, ecotechnic, etc, are derived from Sir Patrick Geddes. Oddly enough, both Patrick Geddes, an early post-traditionalist and Le Corbusier, a fundamentalist modernist in architecture, succeeded in implementing their biggest projects in India. Geddes worked for the princes of British India, and Corbusier worked for Nehru in post-colonial India.

Raja Rao often challenges younger Indians by asking, "How can you modernize India?" For him India can be India only if it remains classical. A classical civilization survives modernity by digesting it, by becoming post-traditional. Certainly Raja Rao's protagonists are post-traditional.

I have deliberately chosen the cumbersome phrase post-traditional to characterize Indian culture in the second half of the twentieth century. Two reasons exist for my decision. Firstly, the Orientalist construction of India requires that it be traditional, in all its Orientalist connotations. There can be no modern without the traditional. An enduring civilization does not mind being a wet-nurse, an ayah, so to speak, for the modern, thus explaining the currency of Orientalist constructions of India within India. However, the use of post-traditional should also suggest a weaning away from that modernizing, imperialist historiography. The phrase post-traditionalism also parodies and teases postmodernism in order to relativize the all-consuming discourse of the modern. Needless to say, unlike postmodernist narcissism, post-traditionalism does not explain itself to itself as post-traditionalism. It faces itself in the mirror much more maturely and securely in the knowledge of its durability and originality. Post-traditionalism is original in the sense of being able to go to the origin. Unlike post modernist which indulges in salvage anthropology, post-traditionalism is a paradigm for survival and endurance.

The INSAT, the Jaipur Foot, and the Aranmula mirror all exemplify post-traditionalism. The simultaneous thriving of such diverse technological traditions testifies to yet another important characteristic of post-traditionalism. Like postmodernism, it too is a pastiche of diverse cultural styles, but a more natural and more tolerant ensemble of lifestyles. Post-traditionalism results when several "Great Traditions," to use a phrase of Robert Redfield, are allowed to meet and interact. This febrile meeting of several civilizations produces, as might be expected, a lush cultural ecology, sustaining multiple cultures. Sensitivity to context, another feature of post- traditional cultures, enables the nourishment of cultural, technological, and economic diversity. As Vikram Sarabhai argued so elegantly, the artificial satellite is indeed one of the most appropriate technologies available to the Indian peasant today. Thus in the context of post-traditional India, modernist, hierarchical categories such as high technology, appropriate technology, and traditional technology are rendered obsolete.

To conclude, one goes to Benaras, especially if one feels like a Hindu. If you don't make it there yourself, you at least pray that your son or grandson will take your, yes, your ashes, to Benaras and immerse them in the Ganges, where the many merge into the one and thus there is neither pariah nor Prime Minister. Even Nehru, secularism-espousing, superstition-denouncing Prime Minister Nehru, had his ashes dissolved in the Ganga, though the only verses he knew of Mother Ganga were composed by Mohammed Iqbal. But then the Mother is forgiving and reminds us that death is no conclusion, only the death of death is and thus death is death, remembered like a mirror; no more or no less. How can it be otherwise once you comprehend action and agency? Every end is only a beginning till It lets you see seeing and thus annihilate the terror of time and be seeingness; pure and simple. And suppose you acknowledge that death is like getting a new wardrobe, would you then panic and conclude hastily? Why, indeed why, the temptation to take shortcuts of technology – mindless automation, mechanization, and computerization – when you have all the time in this world, for how can you die, I ask, how can you die to yourself unless and until all your desires are fulfilled? And pray, of what use is the super-fast, many-laned expressway, if all it does is trap you in a sclerotic traffic jam?

A conclusion is true only when kha, zero, is seen to be ananta, infinity, that is, endings dissolve beginnings, and the son is the father of the father, thus leaving one nowhere and nowhen that is always everywhere. Therefore, the Ramayana ends (well, sort of) in the Post-Ramayana, embedded like a shining gem in ornate golden filigree. Thus stories beget history-begetting stories and as long as you honour the story-teller with coconut and betel-leaf, he will have sons and grandsons who will hold on to the tail of the air-borne elephant and tame wonderful, feral stories, and thus the parayanam, the discourse, will course past time and upper atmosphere into outer space. INSAT will telecast the Ramayana for many, many weeks and keep Indologists scared but employed.

Otherwise how will they make a living, for jobs are scarce and the labour ministers of the G7 countries conferred with their finance ministers in Detroit and came to the disheartening conclusion that the G7 suffered from structural unemployment and not a temporary one. At least the Sinologists speak and write Chinese, a language difficult to master, a language few Americans know. Furthermore, China's trade surplus with the United States continues to explode. But the Indologists may only read Sanskrit, Pali, Tamil, or Marathi and of what use is that when English is the language of India.

How did that happen? India felt English to be an Indo-European language and thus a younger sister to Sanskrit and a foreign-born-cousin, so to speak, of Hindi, and nurtured it even after the British left. Oddly enough once the British left, English grew to be loved even more, befitting a fatherless child, and with the belief that:

> Truth ... is not the monopoly of the Sanskrit language. Truth can use any language, and the more universal, the better it is ... And so long as the English language is universal, it will always remain Indian ... It would then be correct to say as long as we are Indian – that is, not nationalists, but truly Indians of the Indian psyche – we shall have the English language with us and amongst us, and not as a guest or friend, but as one of our own, of our caste, our creed, our sect and our tradition.[17]

Then again you find India claiming that it is the largest Anglophone society. Furthermore, in America, expatriate Indian professors of industrial management brag that India has the largest scientific and technological manpower in the world. "We are just the surplus thrown into the sea," one management expert said, only half-jokingly, speaking of his immigration to America. Under such circumstances, what can an Indologist do to survive a structural recession other than picking up a comical Indian accent for voice-overs on The Simpsons?

The truth of truth is that structural unemployment is but a symptom of an industrial revolution. The first industrial revolution exported its violence and thus descended a Gandhi in his hand-woven loin-cloth to speak at the Round Table Conference and to commiserate with the textile mill workers of Lancaster. If you remember, Gandhi's famous charkha, the spinning wheel, the wheel of life, was re-designed by a Polish-born Jewish electrical engineer searching India for a guru. Wherefrom will a Gandhi arise to comfort the dehumanized detritus of Detroit or Flint, Michigan? Will Gandhi follow Ishi? What might happen if a Mahatma were to meet an Ishi in Minnesota? Maybe the Rockefeller Foundation will be magnanimous as ever, and underwrite such a summit, and then the buffalo shall roam the prairie yet again, and the agricultural subsidies thus saved will reform schools. In the meanwhile, what can death do but die?

May the bison be Benaras-born! May the Raincloud of Dharma ever shower peace and prosperity on all beings, sentient and insentient! Peace! Peace! Peace![18]

Notes

1. This chapter is inspired by Raja Rao's powerful essays on Indian poetics. See Part II of *The Meaning of India* (New Delhi: Vision Books, 1997). Patrick M Malone's elegant monograph, *The Skulking Way of War: Technology and Tactics Among the New England Indians* (Baltimore: Johns Hopkins U P, 1991), points out the continuities in American military strategy that reach back to the Indian wars of the seventeenth century. John McPhee, "Irons in the Fire," *New Yorker* LXIX, 43 (20 Dec 1993): 94, reports with usual charm on cattle-rustling in the American west today.
2. Robert Venturi, *Learning from Las Vegas* (Cambridge, MA: MIT P, 1972).
3. Fredric Jameson, *Postmodernism, Or, the Cultural Logic of Late Capitalism.* (Durham: Duke UP, 1991). Gadgil and Guha, *This Fissured Land: An Ecological History of India* (Delhi: Oxford UP,1992).
4. Agnes Tabah, Native American Collections and Repatriation, (Washington, D C: American Association of Museums, 1992).

5. William McNeil, "The Eccentricity of the Wheel." Hugh Kenner, *The Mechanic Muse*. (New York: Oxford UP, 1987). Richard Bulliet, *The Camel and the Wheel*. (Cambridge, MA: Harvard UP, 1975).
6. Raja Rao, *The Meaning of India*. The 5th century linguist, Bhartrhari, and Benjamin Lee Whorf are two theorists of language I have relied on extensively.
7. Benjamin Lee Whorf, "Language, Mind, and Reality." (1941), in *Language, Thought, and Reality* (Cambridge, MA: Technology P of MIT, 1956).
8. Raja Rao, *The Meaning of India*.
9. Sankara on Patanjali Yoga Sutras. Translation excerpted from Trevor Leggett, *The Complete Commentary by Sankara on the Yoga Sutras: A Full Translation of the Newly Discovered Text* (London: Kegan Paul, 1990): 126.
10. Eugene S Ferguson, *Engineering and the Mind's Eye* (Cambridge, MA: MIT P, 1992).
11. Op cit Whorf, 1-60.
12. Maryla Falk, *Nama Rupa and Dharma Rupa* (Calcutta: U of Calcutta, 1943).
13. Paul Valéry, *Introduction to the Method of Leonardo da Vinci*, 41.
14. The most elegant essay on Indian science, technology and medicine to date is that of Stella Kramrisch, "Natural Science and Technology in Relation to Cultural Patterns and Social Practices in India," in *Philosophy and Culture: East and West*, ed Charles A Moore (Honolulu: U of Hawaii P, 1962).
15. David Pye, *The Nature and Art of Workmanship* (Cambridge, MA: Cambridge UP, 1968).
16. Gregory Clancy, Dissertation in progress, MIT. Also see the unpublished PhD dissertation of Eric Schatzberg, "Ideology and Technical Change: The Choice of Materials in American Aircraft Design Between the World Wars," U of Pennsylvania, 1990.
17. Raja Rao, "The Caste of English," in *Awakened Conscience: Studies in Commonwealth Literature*, Ed C D Narasimhaiah (Delhi: Sterling, 1978): 421.
18. R. Srinivasan, "Templating Contempt: The Cold War Career of William Norman Broswn." Manuscript, 1993.

PRESENTATION OF THE SAHITYA AKADEMI FELLOWSHIP TO RAJA RAO

Raja Rao with the participants at the Word As Mantra Seminar at the University of Texas at Austin, 1997.

PHOTO COURTESY: PROF C. D. NARASIMHAIAH

U R ANANTHA MURTHY

RAJA RAO

Sri Raja Rao, on whom the Sahitya Akademi is conferring its highest honour of Fellowship today, is one of the most distinguished writers of English fiction in India whose contributions have taken the Indian novel in English to rare spiritual heights.

Accepting the much-coveted Neustadt Prize from the University of Oklahoma in 1988, Sri Raja Rao said, "I am a man of silence. And words emerge from that silence with light, of light, and light is sacred... The writer or the poet is he who seeks back the common word to its origin of silence, in order that the manifested word become light." It is this awareness that has given Raja Rao's works the quality of prayers.

His first novel, *Kanthapura*, was published from London in 1938, followed by *The Cow of the Barricades and Other Stories*. Raja Rao's comments on these early works are revealing. "Starting from the humanitarian and romantic perspective of man in *Kanthapura* and *The Cow of the Barricades* – both deeply influenced by Mahatma Gandhi's philosophy of nonviolence – I soon came to the metaphysical novels,

The Serpent and the Rope and *The Cat and Shakespeare*, based on the Vedantic conception of illusion and reality. My main interest increasingly is in showing the complexity of the human condition (that is, the reality of man is beyond his person) and in showing the symbolic construct of any human expression. All words are hierarchic symbols, almost mathematical in precision, on and of the unknown."

E M Forster considered *Kanthapura* to be the best novel ever written in English by an Indian. Not the least of its merits is the picture it gives of life in one of the innumerable villages that are the repositories of India's ancient but living culture. In vivid detail, Rao describes the daily activities, the religious observances and the social structure of the community, and he brings to life in his pages a dozen or more unforgettable individual villagers. The novel is political on a superficial level, in that it chronicles a revolt against an exploitative plantation manager and the police who support him. But more profoundly, it traces the origins of the revolt to an awakening of the long dormant Indian soul rather than to the activities of the Congress party. One of the young men of the village, while away, undergoes a mystical conversion to Satyagraha, and returns to incite his fellow villagers to civil disobedience. He arouses in them not only a sense of social wrong but, more importantly, a religious fervour which proves to be the true source of their strength against the oppressors.

If *Kanthapura* is a novel in which the reader's interest is held mainly by its action and characters, *The Serpent and the Rope* and *The Cat and Shakespeare* are metaphysical novels in which plot, setting and even characters are of secondary interest. Semi-autobiographical, *The Serpent and the Rope* records the disintegration of a marriage, mainly on philosophical grounds, of a very scholarly Indian Brahmin and a French woman professor. The union flounders on the incompatibility of the Brahmin's Vedantic conviction that "Reality is my Self" and the wife's Western belief – even though she has become a Buddhist – that the evidence of our senses is based on an objective reality outside ourselves. "The world is either unreal or real – the serpent or the rope," the Brahmin assures his wife. "There is no in-between-the-two ..." The intellectual demands that Raja Rao, roaming at large through world history and among the religions, philosophies, and literatures of Europe and Asia, makes upon his readers are unequalled in any modern novel since Thomas Mann's *The Magic Mountain*. He quotes at length from a bewildering assortment of languages like Sanskrit, Latin, Provencal, Italian, Old French and other tongues.

The Cat and Shakespeare is much shorter and lighter in tone, though scarcely less metaphysical. The subject of its probings is the problem of individual destiny, and the solution is conveyed through an odd analogy offered by a government clerk: "Learn the way of the kitten. Then you are saved. Allow the mother cat, sir, to carry you." Raja Rao here exploits the Vedantic idea of the world being a play – lila – of the Absolute, and the result is a hilarious comedy that does not even spare Shakespeare and his language.

In *Comrade Kirillov*, Raja Rao exposes communism as ideologically alien to the Indian tradition. He does not hide his preference for the Gandhism that he considers to be the next political system of the world. *The Chessmaster and His Moves* is firmly rooted in the Indian metaphysical tradition that it seeks to illuminate in the form of an epic novel encompassing three countries – India, England and France – besides the fourth one, of the human mind. Structured as a bhashya on the esoteric knowledge of India often expressed in the terse, aphoristic style characteristic of such commentaries, totally indigenous in the narrative pattern that collapses a number of stories as in Bana's *Kadambari* or the *Vikramaditya Tales*, *The Chessmaster and His Moves* reveals the great Upanishadic truth of tat twam asi from the metaphysical position of Advaita Vedanta. The characters here seem to comprise a scale of spiritual awareness in terms of deliverance.

The whole oeuvre of Raja Rao is notable for seriousness of purpose, profundity of thought, a flair for vivid presentation of detail and a distinctive and vigorous English prose. He holds: "We cannot write like the English. We should not. We cannot write only as Indians. We have grown to look at the large world as part of us. Our method of expression, therefore, has to be a dialect which will some day prove to be as distinctive and colourful as the Irish or the American." In fact, Raja Rao's own style is as yet the best example of this kind of distinctive expression in Indian fiction in English.

At eighty eight, Rao is one of the most innovative novelists now writing. Departing boldly from the European tradition of the novel he has indigenized it in the process of assimilating material from the Indian literary tradition. He explores the metaphysical basis of writing itself, and of the world, through his works of fiction. His concern is with the human condition rather than with a particular nation or people. Writing to him is sadhana, a form of spiritual growth. That is why he can say that he would go on writing even if he were alone in the world. In appropriating for fiction the domain of metaphysics, Raja Rao has enlarged the potential of the very genre.

For his unquestionable eminence as a fiction writer, the Sahitya Akademi confers its highest honour, the Fellowship, on Raja Rao.

RAJA RAO

ACCEPTANCE SPEECH

I am a proud Indian. It is my karma that has destined me to live more than half my life outside this Punyabhumi. India indeed is the land of the ultimate value. The Truth. Hence we can believe and shout Satyameva Jayate.

My dream would have been to write in that luminous and precise language Sanskrit, the richest vak in the world. The Sanskrit Dictionary, when it is completed, I am told, would be in about one hundred volumes. But destiny has forced me to learn English – my primary school teachers were all English or Anglo-Indian – and then it was a struggle with my father to go back to a little Sanskrit. It was only in this wise and rich language that I would have liked to have written. Alas it has not been so. But Kannada, my mother tongue, which historians tell me was alive in the Third Century before Christ – it is the language belonging to the Hoysala Land – is what I should have written in. But my karma made me live outside of Karnataka – I was going to say Mysore! – and my Kannada was a babble. I tried and failed writing in it. Thus English it had to be.

The only virtue of English is that it is an Indo-European tongue. An excellent English Dictionary published in America sometime ago has over ninety pages right at the end, to indicate the European tongue, and the Indo-European roots of those given words. And often those roots are the same or similar to those of our Sanskrit.

Thus, though exiled, my country ever and ever is the sacred land, Bharathavarsha. And the honour that the Sahitya Akademi has bestowed on me, in electing me a fellow of this august body, is to show that I am not such a renegade as I might have seemed.

Thus my deepest gratitude goes to you, for your generous gesture.

However, to have been born in India and not have written in Sanskrit, or at least in Kannada is, believe me, an acute humiliation. But I still dream of writing in Sanskrit – one day! May those of you who have given me this honour deeply wish that my dream be achieved. Let my hand and head be blessed by the Mother of vak, the vakdevi, that I achieve this one day.

I deeply thank, once again, the Sahitya Akademi, for having given me the honour of making me a fellow of your unique organization. Namaste!

RAJA RAO: A CHRONOLOGY

COMPILED BY R PARTHASARATHY

1908   Raja Rao: Born on November 8 in Hassan, Mysore, India.

1912   Mother, Gauramma, passes away.

1915   Enters Madarsa-i-Aliya in Hyderabad.

1925   Graduates from the Madarsa.

1926   Studies English with Eric Dickinson and French with Jack Hill for a year at the Aligarh Muslim University, Aligarh, United Provinces.

1927   Continues studies at Nizam's College, Hyderabad.

1929   Graduates with a Bachelor of Arts degree in English and History. Is invited by Sir Patrick Geddes to the College des Ecossais, Montpellier. Receives Asiatic Scholarship for study abroad awarded by the government of Hyderabad. Travels to France to begin studies in French language and literature at the University of Montpellier.

1931   Begins writing, in Kannada, for the periodical *Jaya Karnataka* (Dharwar). Researches at the Sorbonne for the next three years on the Indian influence on Irish literature under the supervision of Louis Cazamian.

1932   Appointed to the editorial board of *Mercure de France* (Paris), a position he held until 1937.

1933   Returns to India to live in Pandit Taranath's ashram in Tungabhadra, Madras Presidency. His first stories published: the French versions of "Javni" in *Europe* (Paris) and of "Akkayya" in *Cahiers du Sud* (Paris). "Javni" is published in *Asia* (New York).

1934   Tthe French version of "A Client" is published in *Mercure de France*, and "In Khandesh" in *Adelphi* (London).

1935   "The True Story of Kanakapala: Protector of Gold" is published in *Asia*.

1937	The French version of "The Little Gram Shop" is published in *Vendredi* (Paris).
1938	The first novel, *Kanthapura*, is published in London, and "The Cow of the Barricades" in *Asia*.
1939	Meets Sri Aurobindo in his ashram in Pondicherry. Lives in Ramana Maharshi's ashram in Tiruvannamalai, Madras Presidency. Edits, with Ahmed Ali, the periodical *Tomorrow* (Bombay) until 1940.
1940	Father, H V Krishnaswami, passes away.
1942	Lives for six months in Mahatma Gandhi's ashram in Sevagram, Central Provinces. Is active in an underground movement against the British.
1943	Meets Sri Atmananda Guru in Tiruvananthapuram, Travancore.
1944	"Narsiga" is published in *Horizon* (Bombay).
1947	*The Cow of the Barricades and Other Stories*, and the Indian edition of *Kanthapura* is published in Madras.
1948	Returns to France.
1950	Visits the USA.
1953	"India – A Story" is published in *Encounter* (London).
1958	Travels in India with Andre Malraux, de Gaulle's emissary to Nehru.
1959	"The Cat" is published in *Chelsea Review* (New York).
1960	*The Serpent and the Rope* is published in London.
1963	"Nimka" and "The Policeman and the Rose" are published in *The Illustrated Weekly of India* (Bombay). Visits Yaddo, Saratoga Springs, Upstate New York. The American editions of *Kanthapura* and *The Serpent and the Rope* are published in New York.
1964	Receives the Sahitya Akademi Award for *The Serpent and the Rope*.
1965	*The Cat and Shakespeare: A Tale of Modern India* is published in New York, and the French translation of *Comrade*

	Kirillov in Paris.
1966	Begins teaching Indian philosophy during the Fall semesters at the University of Texas at Austin.
1968	The Indian edition of *The Serpent and the Rope* is published in India.
1969	Awarded the Padma Bhushan by the government of India.
1971	The Indian edition of *The Cat and Shakespeare* is published.
1972	Named a Fellow of the Woodrow Wilson International Center for Scholars, Washington, DC.
1976	*Comrade Kirillov* is published in English in New Delhi.
1978	*The Policeman and the Rose: Stories* is published in India.
1979	Hungarian translation of *Kanthapura* is published.
1980	Retires as Professor Emeritus of Philosophy from the University of Texas at Austin. The Malayalam translation of *The Cat and Shakespeare*, one of two novels of his to be translated into an Indian language, is puiblished in Kottayam, Kerala.
1984	Elected an Honorary Fellow of the Modern Language Association of America. Visits Japan in the same year.
1988	*The Chessmaster and His Moves* is published in India. Named Tenth Laureate of the Neustadt International Prize for Literature by a panel of writers representing ten nations (February). Receives Neustadt Prize in a formal public ceremony at the University of Oklahoma at Norman (June). The Autumn issue of *World Literature Today* is dedicated to his work.
1989	*On the Ganga Ghat* (stories) is published in India.

Raja Rao, Paris 1986

1997   *The Meaning of India* (essays) is published in India. The Hindi translation of *The Serpent and the Rope* is published in India.

1997   Presented with the Sahitya Akademi Fellowship, India's highest literary honour, at a one-day public symposium on his works, "Word as Mantra: The Art of Raja Rao," organized by the Center for Asian Studies, The University of Texas at Austin (March).

1998   *The Great Indian Way: A Life of Mahatma Gandhi* is published in India on the occasion of the fiftieth anniversary of India's Independence.

RAJA RAO: SELECTED BIBLIOGRAPHY (1931-1998)

COMPILED BY R PARTHASARATHY

1. FICTION

Kanthapura. London: Allen and Unwin, 1938. Bombay: Oxford UP, Champak Library, 1947; Educational edition, 1963. New York: New Directions, 1963. viii + 244 pages. Westport, CT: Greenwood, 1977. (Novel.)

The Cow of the Barricades and Other Stories. Madras: Oxford UP, Champak Library, 1947. vii + 181 pages.

The Serpent and the Rope. London: John Murray, 1960. New York: Pantheon Books, 1963. Delhi: Hind Pocket Books, Orient Paperbacks, 1968. Westport, CT: Greenwood, 1976. Delhi: Oxford UP, Educational edition, 1978. New York: Overlook, 1986. 407 pages. (Novel.)

The Cat and Shakespeare: A Tale of Modern India. New York: Macmillan, 1965. Delhi: Hind Pocket Books, Orient Paperbacks, 1971. 117 pages. (Novella.)

Comrade Kirillov. New Delhi: Vision Books, Orient Paperbacks, 1976. 132 pages. (Novella.)

The Policeman and the Rose: Stories. Delhi: Oxford UP, Three Crowns Books, 1978. xvi + 140 pages.

The Chessmaster and His Moves. New Delhi: Vision Books, 1988. 735 pages. (Novel.)

On the Ganga Ghat. New Delhi: Vision Books, 1989. 131 pages. New Delhi: Orient Paperbacks, 1993. 127 pages. (Stories.)

2. NONFICTION

The Meaning of India. New Delhi: Vision Books, 1996. 204 pages. (Essays.)
The Great Indian Way: A Life of Mahatma Gandhi. New Delhi: Vision Books, 1998. 480 pages. (Biography.)

3. BOOKS EDITED BY RAO

Changing India: An Anthology. Ed Raja Rao and Iqbal Singh. London: Allen and Unwin, 1939.

Whither India? Ed Raja Rao and Iqbal Singh. Bombay: Padma Publications, 1948.

Soviet Russia: Some Random Sketches and Impressions by Jawaharlal Nehru. Ed

Raja Rao. Bombay: Chetana, 1949.

4. CONTRIBUTIONS TO BOOKS

"Recollections of E M Forster." *E M Forster: A Tribute with Selections from His Writings on India*. Ed K Natwar-Singh. New York: Harcourt, Brace, and World, 1964. 15-32.
"The Caste of English." *Awakened Conscience: Studies in Commonwealth Literature*. Ed C D Narasimhaiah. Delhi: Sterling, 1978. 420-22.
"The Cave and the Conch." *The Eye of the Beholder: Indian Writing in English*. Ed Maggie Butcher. London: Commonwealth Institute, 1983. 44-45.

5. CONTRIBUTIONS TO PERIODICALS (FICTION)

"Javni." *Asia*. New York (Nov 1933): Page numbers not available (na).
"Akkayya." *Cahiers du Sud*. Paris (Dec 1933): na (French version).
"A Client." *Mercure de France*. Paris (Aug 1934): 31-48. (French version).
"In Khandesh." *The Adelphi*. London (Nov 1934): na.
"The True Story of Kanakapala, Protector of Gold." *Asia*. New York (Sept 1935): na.
"The Little Gram Shop." *Vendredi*. Paris (1937): na. (French version).
"The Cow of the Barricades." *Asia*. New York (Aug 1938): na.
"Companions." Broadcast from the Lucknow station of All India Radio in 1941 or 1942. [Publishers' Note to *The Cow of the Barricades and Other Stories*.]
"Narsiga." *Horizon*. Bombay (1944): na.
"India-A Story." *Encounter* 1.2. London (Nov 1953): 59-63.
"The Cat". *Chelsea Review*. New York (Summer 1959): na.
"Nimka." *The Illustrated Weekly of India*. Bombay (19 May 1963): 16-17.
"The Policeman and the Rose." *The Illustrated Weekly of India* Bombay (6 Oct 1963): 36-39.
"Creatures of Benares (1)." *World Literature Today* 62.4. Norman, OK (Autumn 1988): 540-03.
"Creatures of Benares (2)." *World Literature Today* 62.4. Norman, OK (Autumn 1988): 543-46.

VERSE

"Expiation of a Heretic". *Jaya Karnataka* 10.10. Dharwar, India (1932): 718-19. (In Kannada).

NONFICTION

"Pilgrimage to Europe." *Jaya Karnataka* 10.1. Dharwar, India (1931): 27-33. (In Kannada.)

"Europe and Ourselves." *Jaya Karnataka* 10.3. Dharwar, India (1931): 204-07. (In Kannada.)

"Romain Rolland, the Great Sage." *Jaya Karnataka* 11.1. Dharwar, India (1933): 46-51. (In Kannada.)

"Pandit Taranath." *Asia*. New York (Jan 1935): 10-15.

"The Premier of Sakuntala." *Asia*. New York (June 1943): 365-68.

"Jupiter and Mars." *Pacific Spectator* 8 (1954): 369-73.

"Varanasi." *The Illustrated Weekly of India*. Bombay (3 Sept 1961): 12-15.

"Trivandrum." *The Illustrated Weekly of India*. Bombay (25 Feb 1962): 12-16.

"Books Which Have Influenced Me." *The Illustrated Weekly of India*. Bombay (10 Feb 1963): 45.

"Andre Malraux Among the Gods of India." *United Asia* 16.2. Bombay (Mar-Apr 1964): 122-28.

"Jawaharlal Nehru: Recollections and Reflections: A Symposium." *The Illustrated Weekly of India*. Bombay (15 Nov 1964): 64-67.

"The Gandhian Way: Replies to a Questionnaire on Gandhi." *The Illustrated Weekly of India*. Bombay (14 Feb 1965): 39.

"The Writer and the Word." *The Literary Criterion* 7.1. Mysore (Winter 1965): 229-31. Rpt in *World Literature Today* 62.4. Norman, OK (Autumn 1988): 538-9.

"Irish Interlude." *The Saturday Review* 49.26. New York (25 June 1966): 21.

"The Climate of Indian Literature Today." *The Literary Criterion* 10.3. Mysore (Winter 1972): 1-7.

"Autobiography: Entering the Literary World." *The Journal of Commonwealth Literature* 13.3. London (Apr 1979): 28-32. Rpt in *World Literature Today* 62.4. Norman, OK (Autumn 1988): 536-8.

6. INTERVIEWS

Bhattacharji, Shobhana. "Interview with Raja Rao." *The Book Review*. New Delhi (Sept-Oct 1982): 63-67.

Jussawalla, Feroza. "Raja Rao." *Interviews with Writers of the Post-Colonial World*. Ed Feroza Jussawalla and Reed Way Dasenbrock. Jackson: UP of Mississippi, 1992. 140-55.

O'Brien, A P. "Meeting Raja Rao." *Prajna*. Golden Jubilee Number. Benaras (1966): 16-17.

Pais, Arthur, and Radhika Radhakrishnan. "Award-winning Raja Rao Likened to Joyce, Proust." *India Abroad*. (27 May 1988): B4-B5.

Parthasarathy, R. "'The Future World Is Being Made in America': An Interview with Raja Rao." *Span*. New Delhi (Sept 1977): 29-30.

R[aman], A S. "A Meeting with Raja Rao Recalled - 1 and 2." *The Illustrated Weekly of India*. Bombay (25 Sept 1966): 13; (25 Oct 1966): 63.

"Ranchan" (pseud Som P Sharma). "A Meeting with Raja Rao." *Thought* 20.28. Delhi (13 July 1968): 14-16; 20.29 (20 July 1968): 14-16; 20.30 (27 July 1968): 14-16; 20.31 (3 Aug 1968): 14-16.

V[asu], S V. "Raja Rao: Face to Face." *The Illustrated Weekly of India*. Bombay (5 Jan 1964): 44-45.

Wohl, Elizabeth. "Raja Rao on America." *Span*. New Delhi (Jan 1973): 35-37.

7. TRANSLATIONS

Samp aur Rassi. Trans Balraj Komal. New Delhi: Sahitya Akademi, 1996. (Trans of *The Serpent and the Rope* into Hindi.)

Poochayum Shakespearum. Trans K Ayyappa Panicker. Kottayam: D C Books, 1980. (Trans of *The Cat and Shakespeare* into Malayalam.)

Kanthapura. Trans Balaban Peter. Hungary: Europa Kvnyvkiado, 1979. (Transl of *Kanthapura* into Hungarian.)

8. BOOKS ON RAO

Bhattacharya, P C. *Indo-Anglian Literature and the Works of Raja Rao*. Delhi: Atma Ram, 1983.

Celly, Anu. *Women in Raja Rao's Novel: A Feminist Reading of* The Serpent and the Rope. Jaipur: Printwell, 1995.

Dey, Esha. *The Novels of Raja Rao: The Theme of Quest*. New Delhi: Prestige Books, in association with the Indian Society for Commonwealth Studies, 1992.

Naik, M K. *Raja Rao*. TWAS 234. New York: Twayne, 1972. Rev ed Bombay: Blackie, 1982.

Narasimhaiah, C D. *Raja Rao*. IWS 4. New Delhi: Arnold-Heinemann, 1973.

Narayan, Shyamala A. *Raja Rao: The Man and His Works*. New Delhi: Sterling, 1988.

Niranjan, Shiva. *Raja Rao: Novelist as Sadhaka*. Ghaziabad, India: Vimal, 1985.

Niven, Alastair. *Truth Within Fiction: A Study of Raja Rao's* The Serpent and the Rope. Calcutta: Writers Workshop, 1987.

Rao, K R. *The Fiction of Raja Rao*. Aurangabad, India: Parimal, 1980.

Sharma, K K, ed. *Perspectives on Raja Rao: An Anthology of Critical Essays*. Ghaziabad, India: Vimal, 1980.

Sharrad, Paul. *Raja Rao and Cultural Tradition*. New Delhi: Sterling, 1988.

Singh, Parminder. *A Semiotic Analysis of Raja Rao's* The Serpent and the Rope. New Delhi: Bahri, 1991.

Srivastava, Narsingh. *The Mind and Art of Raja Rao*. Bareilly, India: Prakash Book Depot, 1980.

9. DISSERTATIONS AND THESES

Gemmill, Janet Powers. "Narrative Technique in the Novels of Raja Rao." Diss U of Wisconsin-Madison, 1972. DAI 33 (1972): 6309A-10A.

Gonzalez, Eva Garcia. "Raja Rao: The Ancient Indian Epics and His Indian Roots". Thesis (MA) U of Wisconsin-Eau Claire, 1990.

Guzman, Richard Ramirez. "Bande Mataram: Nationalism, Personality, and Literary Style in Four Third World Writers [Chinua Achebe, Raja Rao, Bienvenido N Santos, and N V M Gonzalez]." Diss U of Virginia, 1977. DAI 38 (1977): 4180A.

Johns, Timothy Brent. " The Use of the *Ramayana* Epic in the Novels of Raja Rao." Thesis (MA) San Francisco State U, 1994.

Kapur, Anju. "The Rise of the Indian Novel in English." Diss U of Texas at Austin, 1991. DAI 52 (1991): 12A.

Mehan, Uppinder. "The Construction of Self in Selected Novels of Mulk Raj Anand, R K Narayan, and Raja Rao." Diss U of Toronto, 1996. DAI 57 (1996): 08A.

Sharma, Alpana. "Indian Nationalism and Indo-Anglian Literature: A Critical Re-evaluation of Writing Race into the English Language." Diss U of Pittsburgh, 1990. DAI 51 (1990): 11A.

Sharrad, Paul. "Open Dialogue: Metropolitan-Provincial Tensions and the Quest for a Post-Colonial Culture in the Fiction of C J Koch, Raja Rao, and Wilson Harris." Diss Flinders U of South Australia, 1986. DAI 47.6 (1986): 2152A.

Singh, Krishna Seunarine. "An Eternal Quest: The Search for Self in the Novels of Mulk Raj Anand, R K Narayan, Raja Rao, and Salman Rushdie." Thesis (MPhil) U of the West Indies, St Augustine, Trinidad, 1991.

10. ESSAYS ON RAO IN BOOKS AND PERIODICALS

Aithal, S Krishnamoorthy, and Rashmi Aithal. "Interracial and Intercultural Relationships in Raja Rao's *The Serpent and the Rope.*" *The International Fiction Review* 7.2 (Summer 1980): 94-98.

Ali, Ahmed. "Illusion and Reality: The Art and Philosophy of Raja Rao." *The Journal of Commonwealth Literature* 5. London (1968): 16-28.

Amur, G S. "Raja Rao: The Kannada Phase." *The Journal of Karnatak University (Humanities)* 10. Dharwar, India (1966): 40-52.

Belliappa, K C. "The Question of Form in Raja Rao's *The Serpent and the Rope.*" *World Literature Written in English* 24.2. Guelph, Ontario (Autumn 1984): 407-16.

Bhalla, Brij M. "Quest for Identity in Raja Rao's *The Serpent and the Rope.*" Ariel 4.4. London (1973): 95-105.

Curtis, Chantal. "Raja Rao and France." *World Literature Today* 62.4. Norman, OK (Autumn 1988): 595-98.

Das, Elizabeth. "The Choric Element in *Kanthapura.*" *Punjab University Research Bulletin (Arts)* 15.1. Chandigarh, India (Apr 1984): 53-58.

Davies, M Bryn. "Raja Rao's *The Serpent and Rope:* A New Literary Genre?" *The Commonwealth Writer Overseas: Themes of Exile and Expatriation.* Ed Alastair Nivens. Bruxelles: Librairie Marcel Didier S A: 1976. 265-69.

Dayal, P. "The Image of Woman in the Novels of Raja Rao." *Punjab University Research Bulletin (Arts)* 16.1. Chandigarh, India (Apr 1985): 45-53.

—. "Raja Rao and Romain Rolland." *The Literary Criterion* 22.3. Mysore (1987): 65-72.

—. "The Tantric Elements in the Novels of Raja Rao." *The Literary Half-Yearly* 28.1. Mysore (Jan 1987): 105-18.

Desai, S K. "Transplantation of English: Raja Rao's Experimentation with English in His Works of Fiction." *Experimentation with Language in Indian Writing in English (Fiction).* Ed S K Desai. Kolhapur, India: Shivaji University, Department of English, 1974. 1-32.

Dimock, Edward C, Jr."The Garden Wall Between Worlds [A review of *The Cat and Shakespeare*]." *Saturday Review* 48.3. New York (16 Jan 1965): 27-28.

Dissanayake, Wimal. "Questing Self: The Four Voices in *The Serpent and the Rope.*" *World Literature Today* 62.4. Norman, OK (Autumn 1988): 598-602.

Eng, Ooi Boo. "Making Initial Sense of *The Serpent and the Rope.*" *The Journal of Indian Writing in English* 8.1-2. Gulbarga, India (Jan-July 1980): 53-62.

Gemmill, Janet Powers. "Dualities and Non-Duality in Raja Rao's *The Serpent and* the Rope." *World Literature Written in English* 12.6. Arlington, TX (Nov 1973): 247-59.

—. "Elements of the Folktale in Raja Rao's *The Cow of the Barricades.*" *World Literature Written in English* 20.1. Guelph, Ontario (Spring 1981): 149-61.

—. "Initiate Meets Guru: *The Cat and Shakespeare and Comrade Kirillov.*" *World Literature Today* 62.4. Norman, OK (Autumn 1988): 611-16.

—. "*Kanthapura*: India en route to Independence." *CEA Critic* 44.4. College Station, TX (May 1982): 30-38.

—. "Raja Rao's *The Cow of the Barricades:* Two Stories" ["Javni," and "A Client".] *The Journal of South Asian Literature* 13.1-4. East Lansing, MI (1977-78): 23-30.

—. "Raja Rao: Three Tales of Independence" ["Narsiga," "In Khandesh," and "The Cow of the Barricades".] *World Literature Written in English* 15. Arlington, TX (1976): 135-41.

—. "Rhythm in *The Cat and Shakespeare.*" *Literature East & West* 13.1-2. Austin, TX (June 1969): 27-42.

—. "The Transcreation of Spoken Kannada in Raja Rao's *Kanthapura.*" *Literature East & West* 18.2-4. Austin, TX (Mar 1974): 191-202.

Gorlier, Claudio. "See What I Am: The Figure of Beatrice in *The Serpent and the Rope.*" *World Literature Today* 62.4. Norman, OK (Autumn 1988): 606-09.

Gowda, H H Anniah. "Phenomenal Tradition: The Case of Raja Rao and Wilson Harris." *Bulletin of the Association for Commonwealth Literature and Language Studies* 9 (1972): 28-48.

Guzman, Richard R. "The Saint and the Sage: The Fiction of Raja Rao." *The Virginia Quarterly Review* 56.1. Charlottesville, VA (Winter 1980): 32-50.

Harrex, S C. "Typology and Modes: Raja Rao's Experiments in Short Story." *World Literature Today* 62.4. Norman, OK (Autumn 1988): 595-98.

Harris, Wilson. "Raja Rao's Inimitable Style and Art of Fiction." *World Literature Today* 62.4. Norman, OK (Autumn 1988): 587-90.

Isaac, Shanty. "Two French Elements in *The Serpent and the Rope.*" *The Journal of Karnataka University (Humanities)* 18. Dharwar, India (1974): 138-47.

Jamkhandi, S R. "*The Cat and Shakespeare:* Narrator, Audience, and Message." *The Journal of Indian Writing in English* 7.2. Annamalainagar, India (1979): 24-41.

Kachru, Braj B. "Toward Expanding the English Canon: Raja Rao's 1938 Credo for Creativity." *World Literature Today* 62.4. Norman, OK (Autumn 1988): 582-86.

Kantak, V Y. "The Language of *Kanthapura.*" *The Indian Literary Review* 3. New Delhi (Apr 1985): 15-24.

—. "Raja Rao's *Kanthapura.*" *Chandrabhaga* 13. Cuttack, India (Summer 1985): 35-49.

Karnani, Chetan. "From Sense to Nonsense: The Case of Raja Rao." *Thought* 26.32. Delhi (17 Aug 1974): 15.

Kaul, R K. "*The Serpent and the Rope* as a Philosophical Novel." *The Literary Criterion* 15.2. Mysore (1980): 32-43.

Knippling, Alpana Sharma. "R K Narayan, Raja Rao, and Modern English Discourse in Colonial India." *Modern Fiction Studies* 39. West Lafayette, IN (Spring 1993): 169-86.

Krishna Rao, A V. *The Indo-Anglian Novel and the Changing Tradition: A Study of the Novels of Mulk Raj Anand, Kamala Markandaya, R K Narayan, and Raja Rao, 1930-64.* Mysore: Rao and Raghavan, 1972. 107-33.

Larson, Charles R. "Revolt and Rebirth, Cultural Renewal: Raja Rao's *Kanthapura* [and] Kamala Markandaya's *Two Virgins.*" *The Novel in the Third World.* Ed Charles R Larson. Washington, DC: Inscape, 1976. 131-51.

Lehmann, W P. "The Quality of Presence." *World Literature Today* 62.4. Norman, OK (Autumn 1988): 578-82.

Lewis, Robin Jared. "National Identity and Social Consciousness in Modern Indian Literature." *Problems in National Literary Identity and the Writer as Social Critic.* Ed Anne Paolucci. Whitestone, NY: Griffon House, 1980. 38-42.

Maini, D S. "Raja Rao's Vision, Values and Aesthetic." *Commonwealth Literature: Problems of Response.* Ed C D Narasimhaiah. Madras: Macmillan, 1981. 64-89.

Mani, Laxmi. "Voice and Vision in Raja Rao's Fiction." *South Asian Review* 4. Jacksonville, FL (1980): 1-11.

Mathur, O P. "The East-West Theme in *Comrade Kirillov.*" *New Literature Review* 4. Armidale, NSW, Australia (1978): 25-29.

McCutchion, David. "The Novel as Sastra" [A review of *The Serpent and the Rope*]. *Writers Workshop Miscellany* 8. Calcutta (Sep-Oct 1961): 91-99. Rpt *in Indian Writing in English: Critical Essays.* David McCutchion. Calcutta: Writers Workshop, 1969. 69-82. Rpt in *Considerations.* Ed Meenakshi Mukherjee. Columbia, MO: South Asia Books 1977. 90-101.

Moorty, S S. "Beyond the Gandhian Dimension: Mythical and Folkloric Elements in *Kanthapura.*" *The Commonwealth Novel in English* 5.1. Bluefield, WV (Spring 1992): 20-26.

Mukherjee, Meenakshi. "Raja Rao's Shorter Fiction." *Indian Literature* 10.3. New Delhi (1967): 66-76.

—. *The Twice Born Fiction: Themes and Techniques of the Indian Novel in English.* New Delhi: Arnold-Heinemann, 1971. 89-94, 139 45.

Muller, Ulrich, and William C McDonald. "Tristan in Deep Structure: Raja Rao's *The Serpent and the Rope* (1960)-A Paradigmatic Case of Intercultural Relations." *Tristania: A Journal Devoted to Tristan Studies* 12.1-2. Chattanooga, TN (Autumn-Spring 1986-87): 44-47.

Nagarajan, S. "An Indian Novel." [A review of *The Serpent and the Rope.*] *The Sewanee Review* 72.3. Sewanee, TN (Summer 1964): 512-17.

—. "Little Mother in *The Serpent and the Rope.*" *World Literature Today* 62.4. Norman, OK (Autumn 1988): 609-11.

—. "A Note on Myth and Ritual in *The Serpent and the Rope.*" *The Journal of Commonwealth Literature* 7.1. London (1972): 45 48.

Naik, M K. "*The Chessmaster and His Moves.*" [A review of *The Chessmaster and His Moves.*] *Indian Literature* 32.2 New Delhi (1989): 173-78.

—. "*On the Ganga Ghat.*" [A review of *On the Ganga Ghat.*] Indian Literature 33.2. New Delhi (1990): 151-55.

Narasimhaiah, C D. "National Identity in Literature and Language: Its Range and Depth in the Novels of Raja Rao." *National Identity.* Ed K L Goodwin. London and Melbourne: Heinemann Educational Books, 1970. 153-68.

Narayan, Shyamala A. "Ramaswamy's Erudition: A Note on Raja Rao's *The Serpent and the Rope.*" *Ariel* 14.4. Calgary, Alberta (Oct 1983): 6-15.

—. "Woman in Raja Rao's Fiction." *The Literary Criterion* 20.4. Mysore (1985): 35-45.

Narayana Rao, K S. "The Untranslated Translation and Aesthetic Consequences: Indian Fiction in English." *Southern Review* 8.3. Adelaide (1975): 189-204.

Niranjan, Shiva. "The Nature and Extent of Gandhi's Impact on the Early Novels of Mulk Raj Anand and Raja Rao." *Commonwealth Quarterly* 3.11. Mysore (1979): 36-46.

Niven, Alastair. "Any Row Over Rao?" *Commonwealth Newsletter* 6. London (1974): 34-35.

Pallan, Rajesh K. *Myths and Symbols in Raja Rao and R K Narayan: A Select Study.* Jalandhar, Punjab: ABS Publications, 1994.

Panicker, K Ayyappa. "A Conversation with Raja Rao on *The Cat and Shakespeare.*" *Chandrabhaga* 2. Cuttack, India (1979): 14-18.

—. "The Frontiers of Fiction: A Study of Raja Rao's *The Cat and Shakespeare.*" *The Literary Criterion* 15.1. Mysore (1980): 60-72.

Parameswaran, Uma. "Karma at Work: The Allegory in Raja Rao's *The Cat and*

Shakespeare." *The Journal of Commonwealth Literature* 7. London (July 1969): 107-15.

—. "Shakti in Raja Rao's Novels." *Bulletin of the Association for Commonwealth Literature and Language Studies* 9 (1972): 4-27.

—. "Siva and Shakti in Raja Rao's Novels." *World Literature Today* 62.4. Norman, OK (Autumn 1988): 574-77.

—. *A Study of Representative Indo-English Novelists.* Ghaziabad, India: Vikas, 1976. na

Parthasarathy, R. "The Chessmaster and His Moves: The Novel as Metaphysics." *World Literature Today* 62.4. Norman, OK (Autumn 1988): 561-66.

—. "Tradition and Creativity: Stylistic Innovations in Raja Rao." *Discourse Across Cultures: Strategies in World Englishes.* Ed Larry E Smith. London: Prentice-Hall, 1987. 157-65.

Patil, Chandrasekhar B. "The Kannada Element in Raja Rao's Prose: A Linguistic Study of *Kanthapura.*" *Journal of Karnataka University (Humanities)* 13 (1969): na

Perera, S W. "Towards a Limited Emancipation: Women in Raja Rao's *Kanthapura.*" *Ariel* 23.4. Guelph, Ontario (Oct 1992): 99-110.

Pousse, Michel. "Gandhi in the Novels of Mulk Raj Anand and Raja Rao." *Indian Horizons* 43.4. New Delhi (1994): 209-16.

Raine, Kathleen. "On *The Serpent and the Rope.*" *World Literature Today* 62.4. Norman, OK (Autumn 1988): 603-05.

Raizada, Harish C. "Literature as 'Sadhana': The Progress of Raja Rao from *Kanthapura* to *The Serpent and the Rope.*" *Indo-English Literature: A Collection of Critical Essays.* Ed K K Sharma. Ghaziabad, India: Vimal, 1977. 157-75.

Ram, Atma. "Peasant Sensibility in *Kanthapura.*" *Indo-English Literature: A Collection of Critical Essays.* Ed K K Sharma. Ghaziabad, India: Vimal, 1977. 193-200.

"Ranchan" (pseud Som P Sharma). "*The Serpent and the Rope* – India Made Real." *The Illustrated Weekly of India.* Bombay (13 Mar 1966): 45-47; (3 Apr 1966): 33-35; (10 Apr 1966): 33-35.

Rao, A Ramakrishna. "Kirillov in the First Circle." *The Literary Endeavour* 6.1-4. Nizamabad, India (1985): 45-54.

Rao, J Srihari. "Images of Truth: A Study of Raja Rao's *The Cat and Shakespeare.*" *The Journal of Indian Writing in English* 5.1. Annamalainagar, India (1977): 36-41.

Ray, Robert. "The Novels of Raja Rao." *Books Abroad* 40.4. Norman, OK (Autumn 1966): 411-14.

Reddy, K Venkata. "An Approach to Raja Rao's *The Cat and Shakespeare*." *World Literature Written in English* 20.2. Guelph, Ontario (Autumn 1981): 337-43.

Sankaran, Chitra. "Misogyny in Raja Rao's *The Chessmaster and His Moves*." *The Journal of Commonwealth Literature* 30.1. Oxford (1995): 87-95.

—. *The Myth Connection: The Use of Hindu Mythology in Some Novels of Raja Rao and R K Narayan*. Ahmedabad: Allied Publishers, 1993.

Sarachchandra, Ediriwira. "Illusion and Reality: Raja Rao as Novelist." *Only Connect: Literary Perspectives East and West*. Ed Guy Amirthanayagam and S C Harrex. Adelaide: Centre for Research in the New Literatures; Honolulu: East-West Center, 1981. 107-17.

Seshachari, Candadai. "The Gandhian Dimension: Revolution and Tragedy in *Kanthapura*." *South Asian Review* 5.2. Jacksonville, FL (July 1981): 82-87.

Shahane, Vasant A. "Raja Rao: *Kanthapura*." *Major Indian Novels: An Evaluation*. Ed N S Pradhan. Atlantic Highlands, NJ: Humanities Press, 1986. 22-40.

—. "Raja Rao's *The Serpent and the Rope* and Patrick White's *The Solid Mandala*: A Comparative Appraisal." *The Laurel Bough: Essays Presented in Honour of Professor M V Rama Sarma*. Ed G Nageswara Rao. Bombay: Blackie, 1983. 177-89.

Sharma, Jatindra Kumar. "Response to Alien Culture in Henry James and Raja Rao: Comparative Observations on *The American* and *The Serpent and the Rope*." *Punjab University Research Bulletin (Arts)* 15.1. Chandigarh, India (Apr 1984): 11-25.

Sharma, Som P. "Raja Rao's Search for the Feminine." *The Journal of South Asian Literature* 12.3. East Lansing, MI (1977): 95-101.

Sharrad, Paul. "Aspects of Mythic Form and Style in Raja Rao's *The Serpent and the Rope*." *The Journal of Indian Writing in English* 12.2. Gulbarga, India (July 1984): 82-95.

—. "Memory, Childhood, and Exile: Self-Representation in Post-Colonial Writing." *World Englishes* 9.2. Oxford (Summer 1990): 137-53.

—. "A Sense of Place in Raja Rao's *The Serpent and the Rope*." *A Sense of Place in the New Literatures in English*. Ed Peggy Nightingale. St. Lucia: U of Queensland P, 1986. 86-96.

Shepherd, R. "The Character of Ramaswamy in Raja Rao's *The Serpent and the Rope*." *New Literature Review* 4. Armidale, NSW, Australia (1978): 17-24.

—."Raja Rao: Symbolism in *The Cat and Shakespeare*." *World Literature Written in English* 14.2. Arlington, TX (Nov 1975): 347-56.

—. "Symbolic Organization in *The Serpent and the Rope*." *Southern Review: An*

Australian Journal of Literary Studies 6. Adelaide (1973): 93-107.

Srinivasa Iyengar, K R. "Raja Rao." *Indian Writing in English*. K R Srinivasa Iyengar. Bombay: Asia Publishing House, 1962. 302-20.

—. "Literature as Sadhana: A Note on Raja Rao's *The Cat and Shakspeare*." *Aryan Path* 40.6. Bombay (June 1969): 301-05.

Taranath, Rajeev. "A Note on the Problem of Simplification." *Fiction and the Reading Public in India*. Ed C D Narasimhaiah. Mysore: U of Mysore, 1967. 205-12.

Tiffin, Helen. "The Word and the House: Colonial Motifs in *The Double Hook* and *The Cat and Shakespeare*." *The Literary Criterion 20.1*. Mysore (1985): 204-26.

Thumboo, Edwin. "Raja Rao: *The Chessmaster and His Moves*." *World Literature Today* 62.4. Norman, OK (Autumn 1988): 567-73.

Verghese, C Paul. "Raja Rao, Mulk Raj Anand, R K Narayan, and Others." *Indian Writing Today* 3.1. Bombay (Jan-Mar 1969): 31-38.

Walsh, William. *Commonwealth Literature*. London: Oxford UP, 1973. 9-11.

—, ed. *Readings in Commonwealth Literature*. Oxford: Clarendon P, 1973. 52-54.

Westbrook, Perry D. "Raja Rao: *Comrade Kirillov* – Marxism and Vedanta." *World Literature Today* 62.4. Norman, OK (1988): 617-20.

—. "Theme and Inaction in Raja Rao's *The Serpent and the Rope*." *World Literature Written in English* 14. Arlington, TX (1975): 385-98.

White, Ray Lewis. "Raja Rao's *The Cat and Shakespeare* in the USA." *The Journal of Indian Writing in English* 7.1. Annamalainagar, India (1979): 24-29.

Williams, Haydn Moore. "Raja Rao's *The Serpent and the Rope* and the Idea of India." *Rule, Protest, Identity: Aspects of Modern South Asia*. Ed Peter G Robb and David D Taylor. Collected Papers on South Asia 1. London: Curzon, 1978. 206-12.

(The compiler thanks Rosemary A Delvecchio and Jennifer Taxman of the Lucy Scribner Library, Skidmore College, for their assistance in the preparation of this bibliography.)

Raja Rao, 1997.

ANNE MORRIS
A RAJA RAO RETROSPECTIVE[*]

Raja Rao leans forward, his eyes intent. "Ask me any questions," says the old, slightly lilting, voice. "Go ahead. You can ask me anything."

This unusual invitation comes from one of India's finest writers in English, the 1988 winner of the prestigious $25,000 Neustadt International Prize for Literature. The books Rao has written and the books by others published in India analyzing his novels, fill two shelves in the Perry Castaneda Library at the University of Texas: *Raja Rao: Man and His Works*, *Indo-Anglian Literature and the Works of Raja Rao*, *Women in Raja Rao's Novel: A Feminist Reading of The Serpent and the Rope*. And so on. Rao knew Gandhi and Nehru. In India he would be, as he puts it, "somewhat important." But he chooses to live in Austin. "Austin has some very beautiful things and a wonderful library at the university. The people here are very simple and kindly people."

John Silber, one of UT's bolder Liberal Arts deans, first recruited Rao to teach Indian philosophy here in the mid-1960's after *The Serpent and the Rope* was published. Except for trips to India and occasional visits elsewhere, the author has been here since. Retired from teaching, the eighty eight year old Rao lives quietly in the same neat West Campus duplex he has rented for thirty years. To him, the years when Silber was here were the best. "He was a difficult man, but a revolutionary."

Rao is in good health. He eats a vegetarian diet; he rises at 6:30 am to meditate; he walks along the river; he works; he meditates some more. He sees few people now – largely only those interested in philosophical discusssion – a group whose numbers he sees as dwindling.

But beginning at 10 am on Monday, the Department of Asian Studies

---

[*] Copyright 1997, *Austin American-Statesman*. Reprinted with permission. The article originally appeared in the *Austin American-Statesman*, Sunday, 23 March, 1997, on the eve of The University of Texas symposium honoring Raja Rao. Anne Morris is with the American-Statesman staff.

at the university will hold a free day-long public symposium at the Harry Ransom Humanities Research Center on his works. "It will be the occasion for the presentation of the Sahitya Akademi Fellowship, India's highest literary award," said Professor Robert Hardgrave, acting director of the Center for Asian Studies. "The president of the Akademi will come from India to make the presentation." Hardgrave adds that Rao – this quiet Austin resident who is a regular on the hike-and-bike trail – is widely regarded as India's greatest writer. Denis de Rougemont, the French philosopher, once said of Rao's major work, "I know nothing in literature that confronts East and West more tenderly, more rigorously." E M Forster, renowned author of *A Passage to India*, described *The Serpent and the Rope* as "perhaps the best novel in English to come from India."

Rao, whose third wife Susan was a UT student in the '70s, says that though he lives in Austin he has in fact never left India. "India is my home; there is no question." Does Rao write better about India, living outside of it?

"No, I don't think so, India is everywhere. Look at my house," he says, glancing at an Indian picture. "Look inside my books in my room. It's all very Indian."

Does he write to translate India for the West, then, as some critics have suggested?

"No. I just do it for myself. I make no concession to the West. Right, Susan?"

His wife of 12 years laughs. "Oh, absolutely. In no way, at any time."

Rao has two sons, both born in Austin but now living in St. Louis and India.

Rao defines the major theme of all his fiction as the search for the truth; man's search for ultimate values. It is a search that has consumed much of his life.

Rao grew up in Mysore, an area of coffee plantations and famous old temples, in the south of India. He was a member of an old and respected Brahmin family. He did not study fiction writing, but came to it naturally. "I wrote as a man of sixteen or seventeen," Rao says. "I wrote in English. I was sent to a very snobbish English school. I learned English from English people in India. I learned Sanskrit much later."

His father was a scholar and professor. But it was from his grandfather, who spoke not a word of English and meditated at length, that Rao got his philosophical bent. "My grandfather started me on the search," he says. "Philosophical inquiry is personal contact. Not merely philosophical thinking. Indian philosophy is thought in the West to be mystical. But it's really logic. Logical and metaphysical."

He went to the Aligarh Muslim University and to Nizam's College, Hyderabad, in India. At the age of nineteen, he went to France, where he studied at the University of Montpellier and later at the Sorbonne. He left France in 1939, fifteen days before the outbreak of World War II. "If I'd been there fifteen days more, I'd not be alive today," he says, because of his opposition to Hitler. "I was just lucky. When I got to India, I went straight to a sage."

"France, to my mind, is still the heart of Western civilization," Rao says. His first wife was a professor of French, and for about thirty years he lived six months in France; six months in India. For a time he considered becoming a monk.

His first novel, *Kanthapura*, about a village in South India affected by the spirit of Gandhi, was published in the United States in 1938. *The Serpent and the Rope* was published here in 1960. Other works include a collection of stories written earlier, *The Cow of the Barricades*, but published in 1947; *The Cat and Shakespeare* in 1965; *Comrade Kirillov* in 1976; *The Chessmaster and his Moves* in 1988. In the years since, Rao had been working on a sequel to this last novel, which has Indian Vedantic philosophy at its core.

"I became a professor here in 1966," Rao says. "I had never taught before. I only had a third-class BA degree. I don't think I ever had a professor with such low qualifications," he smiles. (At the time he was married to Catherine Jones, an actress.)

"In the '60s and '70s the search for values was very remarkable. I was really thinking America would be the greatest nation ..." Rao points out that America had been fascinated by India even earlier. "The 19th century transcendentalists – Thoreau, Whitman, Emerson – were all influenced by India. The pragmatic American, I think, has not got time for India." These days Rao sees less interest in the philosophical. "Most of modern literature is psychological," he says. "There is no search in it. Philosophy began to go down in '78 and '79."

He sees the West in a state of great gestation. "The West has not reached its destiny," he said. Rao feels he has found answers to his philosophical searching through meditation and long study with a guru in India. "I am not a guru," Rao says. "A guru is pure consciousness, a person with no ego," He laughs. "I have an ego. Yes. Still!

PHOTO COURTESY: GIL JAIN

Raja Rao and Susan, University of Oklahoma, 1988

▼▼▼▼▼▼▼▼▼▼▼▼▼▼▼▼▼▼▼▼▼▼▼▼▼▼▼▼▼▼▼

ABOUT THE CONTRIBUTORS

U R ANANTHA MURTHY is a past President of the Sahitya Akademi, and is among India's most distinguished writers. His powerful novel *Samskara*, published in Kannada in 1965 and in English translation in 1976, was critically acclaimed and remains among the most popular of his many works. He has long been associated with the Iowa Writer's Workshop.

BRAJ B KACHRU is Professor of Linguistics at the Center for Advanced Study and Jubilee Professor of Liberal Arts and Sciences. He is also Director of the Center for Advanced Study at the University of Illinois at Urbana-Champaign. His publications include *The Other Tongue: English Across Cultures* (1982), *The Indianization of English* (1983), and *The Alchemy of English* (1986). He has written numerous articles on linguistics, English in India, world Englishes, and on the Kashmiri language and literature. He is a founder and co-editor of *World Englishes*, series editor of *English in the Global Context*, and was associate editor of *The Oxford Companion to the English Language*. He is a past President of the American Association for Applied Linguistics (1984), and was Director of the Linguistics Institute of the Linguistic Society of America (1978).

KATHLEEN RAINE is a distinguished poet, critic and editor of the London-based journal *Temenos: A Review Devoted to the Arts of the Imagination*. Among many honours, she is an Officier de l'Order des Arts et Lettres and Doctor of Literature. Her works of poetry include *Collected Poems* (1956) and *The Oracle of the Heart* (1976).

MAKARAND R PARANJAPE is Associate Professor in the Department of Humanities and Social Sciences at the Indian Institute of Technology, New Delhi. In addition to works of criticism that include *Mysticism in Indian English Poetry* (1988) and *Decolonization and Development: Hind Swaraj Revisioned* (1993), he has two volumes of poems, *The Serene Flame* (1991) and *Playing the Dark God* (1992), a collection of short stories, and a novel, *The Narrator* (1995). With extensive academic publications, Dr Paranjape is also a regular columnist on the literary scene for Indian newspapers.

C D NARASIMHAIAH is the Director of The Literary Criterion Centre for English Studies and Indigenous Arts at Dhvanyaloka, Mysore. Among India's most distinguished literary critics, he has been a visiting Professor and research scholar at leading universities throughout the world. His books include *The Swan and the Eagle* (1969; 1989), *Raja Rao, Novelist* (1973), *The Function of Criticism in India* (1987), *The Indian Critical Scene: Controversial Essays* (1990), and *'N' for Nobody – Autobiography of an English Teacher* (1992).

R PARTHASARATHY is a poet, translator, critic and editor. He is the author of *Rough Passage* (1977), a long poem and editor of *Ten Twentieth-Century Indian Poets* (1976). He has translated into modern English verse the 5th century Tamil epic, *The Tale of an Anklet* (1993), for which he was awarded the 1995 Sahitya Akademi Award for Translation and the 1996 Association for Asian Studies A K Ramanujan Book Prize for Translation. He has been editing the works of Raja Rao since 1974. He is Director of the Program in Asian Studies at Skidmore College, Saratoga Springs, New York.

RAMAN SRINIVASAN is currently Executive Director of the Madras Foundation and also holds a position with Orpheus Multimedia, both in Chennai. He is an alumnus of the Indian Institute of Technology (Chennai) and holds a PhD from the University of Pennsylvania in the History and Sociology of Science. He is a published poet and was drawn to Raja Rao through *The Chessmaster and His Moves*.

ROBERT D KING holds the Audre and Bernard Rapoport Regents Chair of Jewish Studies at the University of Texas at Austin, where he has appointments in the departments of Asian Studies, Linguistics, and

Germanic Studies. He was Dean of the College of Liberal Arts for most of the years between 1976 and 1993. His book, *Nehru and the Language Politics of India*, was published in 1997 by Oxford University Press.

ROBERT L HARDGRAVE, JR, is Temple Professor of the Humanities in Government and Asian Studies at the University of Texas at Austin. As Acting Director of the Center for Asian Studies in 1996-97, he organized the symposium "Word as Mantra: The Art of Raja Rao" and edited the papers for this volume. Author of works on politics and social change in India, he is currently writing a book on the Flemish artist Baltazard Solvyns (1760-1824) and of his etchings portraying the Hindus and their culture.

WINFRED P LEHMANN is the Louann and Larry Temple Centennial Professor Emeritus in Humanities and is Director of the Linguistics Research Center at the University of Texas at Austin. He presented the Nehru Memorial Lecture, New Delhi, in 1981. Among his recent books and monographs are *Die Gegenwaertige Richtung der Indogermanistischen Forschng* (1992), *Historical Linguistics*, 3rd ed (1992), *Theoretical Bases of Indo-European Linguistics* (1993), and *Residues of Pre-Indo-European Active Structure and Their Implications for the Relationships Among the Dialects* (1995).

YAMUNA KACHRU is Professor of Linguistics at the University of Illinois at Urbana-Champaign. She is the author of *An Introduction to Hindi Syntax* (1966), *Aspects of Hindi Grammar* (1980), co-editor of the *Pragmatics and Language Learning* monograph series (1990-94), and has authored numerous works on Hindi grammar, discourse analysis, the interface of language and culture, bilingual lexicography, and English as a world language. She served as Chair of the Committee on Status of Women in Linguistics of the Linguistic Society of America (1985-86).

Katha's Academic Series
BRING YOUR CLASSES ALIVE WITH
Stories, Essays, Criticism
Excellently researched ... innovatively produced

TRANSLATING CASTE

For those who live it, for those who read about it, for those who teach it – this is a volume with a spread of representations of caste in seven modern Indian languages. Four critical commentaries trace the contours of the politics of writing and the issues surrounding cultural idioms loaded with the consciousness of caste. The four overviews of the issue of caste and its prevailing social manifestations by known authorities put the history of caste in critical perspective. An interview with a woman Dalit (backward class) writer completes the pedagogical design of this text.

"... bound to be of interest to readership constituencies outside academia as well ... intelligent and coherent ... recommended to those interested."
– *First City*

Stories by
Arupa Pantangia Kalita, Irathina Karikalan, K P Ramanunni, Mahasweta Devi, Mogalli Ganesh, M T Vasudevan Nair, Narain Singh, Urmila Pawar

Essays, Criticism

EDITED BY
Tapan Basu

Katha's Academic Series
BRING YOUR CLASSES ALIVE WITH
Stories, Essays, Criticism
Excellently researched ... innovatively produced

TRANSLATING PARTITION

This Volume of Stories and essays present the literary and historiographic representations of the Partition of the Indian subcontinent in 1947. The essays analyze critically the events that led up to the Partition, the representation of the Partition in Indian newspapers prior to 1947, and treatment of violence and trauma in Partition literature. The stories and essays explore the Partition and its consequence from the perspective of people's history. The stories of displacement, loss, violence, trauma, uprooting, and rebuilding of individuals and communities ... The question, "Why must we write this history today?" is posed as an important one.

"A commendable volume that attempts to provide a new dimension to the travails of Partition." — Inder Malhotra *Hindustan Times*

Stories by
Manto, Bhisham Sahni, Surendra Prakash
Attia Hossain, Joginder Paul, Kamleshwar
Essays, Criticism
EDITED BY
Tarun K Saint & Ravikant

ABOUT KATHA

Katha, a registered nonprofit organization set up in September 1989, works in the areas of education, publishing and community development and endeavours to spread the joy of reading, knowing and living amongst adults and children. Our main objective is to enhance the pleasures of reading for children and adults, for experienced readers as well as for those who are just beginning to read. Our attempt is also to stimulate an interest in lifelong learning that will help the child grow into a confident, self-reliant, responsible and responsive adult, as also to help break down gender, cultural and social stereotypes, encourage and foster excellence, applaud quality literature and translations in and between the various Indian languages and work towards community revitalization and economic resurgence. The two wings of Katha are **Katha Vilasam** and **Kalpavriksham**.

KATHA VILASAM, the Story Research and Resource Centre, was set up to foster and applaud quality Indian literature and take these to a wider audience through quality translations and related activities like **Katha Books**, **Academic Publishing**, the **Katha Awards** for fiction, translation and editing, **Kathakaar** – the Centre for Children's Literature, **Katha Barani** – the Translation Resource Centre, the **Katha Translation Exchange Programme**, **Translation Contests**. **Kanchi** – the Katha National Institute of Translation promotes translation through **Katha Academic Centres** in various Indian universities, **Faculty Enhancement Programmes** through Workshops, seminars and discussions, **Sishya** – Katha Clubs in colleges, **Storytellers Unlimited** – the art and craft of storytelling and **KathaRasa** – performances, art fusion and other events at the Katha Centre.

KALPAVRIKSHAM, the Centre for Sustainable Learning, was set up to foster quality education that is relevant and fun for children from nonliterate families, and to promote community revitalization and economic resurgence work. These goals crystallized in the development of the following areas of activities. **Katha Khazana** which includes **Katha Student Support Centre**, **Katha Public School**, **Katha School of Entrepreneurship**, **KITES** – the Katha Information Technology and eCommerce School, **Iccha Ghar** – The Intel Computer Clubhouse @ Katha, **Hamara Gaon** and **The Mandals** – Maa, Bapu, Balika, Balak and Danadini, **Shakti Khazana** was set up for skills upgradation and income generation activities comprising the Khazana Coop. **Kalpana Vilasam** is the cell for regular research and development of teaching/learning materials, curricula, syllabi, content comprising **Teacher Training, TaQeEd** – The Teachers Alliance for Quality eEducation. **Tamasha's World!** comprises Tamasha! the Children's magazine, *Dhammakdhum! www.tamasha.org* and ANU – Animals, Nature and YOU!

BE A FRIEND OF KATHA!

If you feel strongly about Indian literature, you belong with us! KathaNet, an invaluable network of our friends, is the mainstay of all our translation related activities. We are happy to invite you to join this ever widening circle of translation activists. Katha, with limited financial resources, is propped up by the unqualified enthusiasm and the indispensable support of nearly 5000 dedicated women and men.

We are constantly on the lookout for people who can spare the time to find stories for us, and to translate them. Katha has been able to access mainly the literature of the major Indian languages. Our efforts to locate resource people who could make the lesser known literatures available to us have not yielded satisfactory results. We are specially eager to find Friends who could introduce us to Bhojpuri, Dogri, Kashmiri, Maithili, Manipuri, Nepali, Rajasthani and Sindhi fiction.

Do write to us with details about yourself, your language skills, the ways in which you can help us, and any material that you already have and feel might be publishable under a Katha programme. All this would be a labour of love, of course! But we do offer a discount of 20% on all our publications to Friends of Katha.

Write to us at –
Katha
A-3 Sarvodaya Enclave
Sri Aurobindo Marg
New Delhi 110 017

Call us at: 2652 4350, 2652 4511
or E-mail us at: info@katha.org

Have you got the Katha Trailblazers

Paul Zacharia

Ashokamitran

Bhupen Khakhar

Indira Goswami

Order directly with us and avail a 20% discount
... and have your books sent to you.

A-3, Sarvodaya Enclave, Sri Aurobindo Marg, New Delhi 110 017   Ph: 2652 4511, 2652 4350
Fax: 2651 4373   •   E-mail: marketing@katha.org   •   www.FictionIndia.com